RELIGION VS. RELATIONSHIP:

Discovering the God
I Always Knew Was There!

BY RANDY HAMMON

Author of *The Safe Money System*

ISBN: 0615475248
ISBN-13: 9780615475240

TABLE OF CONTENTS

ACKNOWLEDGEMENTS

Where does one start in giving thanks for those people whom God has brought across the path of my spiritual journey over these many years? The problem as I look back over the highway of my life's experiences is I am mostly oblivious to God's hand on me during the Journey called life.

Oh, I know He was directing the "Show" in the big sense, but I just can't figure out why He chose this road or that road; this person or that person; this outcome or that outcome.

But I do know that I start with my God-Father as I give thanks to Him for a wonderful, challenging life that has me more excited and expectant at age 59 for the things to come than at any previous time in my life. He indeed "causes all things to work for His good, to those whom He loves and who are called according to His purposes". (Romans 8:28) I didn't say He caused my greatest disappointments, failures, shortcomings — I said His word promises me that in those things He works His purposes for me — in spite of my dumb, stubborn self! Thanks, Pop!

To my dear wife Crystal, I'm so blessed and honored to share with you in the great things that God has done in our lives individually and collectively as a family. The years ahead will be great! Thanks for trusting my spiritual leadership over our boys and our life together. I love you, Baby!

To my sons Brandon, Nolan, Dillon and Dylan, thanks for respecting me, loving me and honoring me— in spite of knowing "what a horse's ass saved by grace" I truly am. Remember that your God-Father loves you, will provide for you, and expects great things out of you as you take your talents and bless others throughout your lives. The King always expects great things from His kids! Conduct yourselves like the Royalty you are! I have enjoyed the transition from your earthly dad to your brother in the Lord— For now, and into Eternity. I love you guys!

To Pastor Steve Hage of the Gathering Church, you are called to a High Anointing to exhort, encourage and enable God's people to be what He has called them to be — His Kingdom ambassadors here on earth, armed with the power of His Holy Spirit, to accomplish the task of kickin' the devil's hind side as the opportunity arises. Your teaching, leadership and friendship is one of God's great blessings to my family and I. Thanks also to your talented wife, Daniele, for her leadership, grace and the ability to keep you in line! I love you, man!

To Pastor Denny Bellesi, my long time pastor of Coast Hills Church (before retirement into your new adventure with Leesa), thanks for over twenty years of encouragement, deep friendship and anointed teaching as God's servant to our family. I love you, and the best is yet to come in our Assignment in His Kingdom on earth!

To my dear brother in the Lord, Rick Bradley, for your love and kinship these 34 years, our bible studies and discussions during our pro baseball years were the foundation for my Journey with God. Today's discussions continue to fuel my soul. May He continue to use you in my life, and in the lives of those He brings across your path. The Bay loves you, Bad Brad!

To my warrior brothers in this spiritual Journey, Buck Barbee, Paul Ednoff, Phil Steffeck, Vic Domines, and Greg Bero, who have stood by me in prayer, encouraged me in my battles, and continue to remind me that it is God to whom all Glory and Praise is due. Look what God has done our lives — in spite of ourselves!!!! I love you all, and look forward to spending the rest of our lives and Eternity together!

To the many men who I still call my brothers from my years at Coast Hills Church, to my current Band of Brothers at the Gathering Church, and to my many friends with whom God has so blessed me over these many years from my pro baseball career, from among my clients and business associates, and my family members— who all played a great part in my development as a man who loves God. You all know who you are, and I'm grateful for you all!

To Michael Gerber, my dear mentor and encourager, for challenging me to Dream Big with the talents God gave me. May God continue to guide and bless you in your Assignment to encourage Dreamers the world over to take their God-given talents to bless others!

And, finally, to Michael Levin, a Jew who loves God and who is loved by God, for your faithful exhortation to me to write this book, and for your God-given inspiration and talent in seeing this effort through to its finish. I love you, and am a blessed man to know you and call you my friend.

FOREWORD

I believe there exists in the heart of every person a longing and yearning for a connection with our Creator. It is what I believe is the driving force behind every season of searching that each one of us has experienced until we discover the gift of grace and authentic relationship with our heavenly Father that Jesus provides! No person walks complete until this relationship is established in their heart.

Our God connection is to be lived from our heart to our heavenly Father's heart. Then our life becomes an extension of God's heart to our sphere of influence in the world. This is a true relationship with God.

Religion is lived from our head and can never fully understand God's heart! As you read this book, my prayer for you is that you will gain perspective and grow in an understanding of the difference between religion and relationship. As Randy shares his story and his thoughts, I trust your relationship with the Lord will increase and your awareness of the inability of man-made religious tradition to answer your heart's cry for relationship with God will become more pronounced.

Enjoy,
Pastor Steve Hage
The Gathering Community Church
Laguna Niguel, CA
www.octhegathering.com

WHY I HOPE YOU READ THIS BOOK

Most Bible-reading Christians are familiar with the Gospel of Mark, chapter 7, which sets forth Jesus' response to the Pharisees, the religious leaders of the Jews, who were more concerned with outward, empty traditional rules instead of having a real, substantial relationship with a loving God.

The problem is that in today's world among many Christian-based religions, there still exists a spirit of the Pharisees.

Have you stepped into a church and felt that the atmosphere was one of enforcing denominational doctrine and rigid performance among the faithful in order to "appease" God?

Have you wondered why religion has made it so hard for you to earn eternal life with Him by emphasizing your need for religious performance?

Have you felt that all you wanted of a church is to shepherd you into a deep, intimate relationship with your God-Father rather than creating a spirit of judgment and shame where God's grace is nowhere to be found.

Religion that is pure is meant to bind the believer to God and to a Godly community of fellow believers. Today, much of Christianity is an empty shell, hijacked by those who are feeding on the religion's carcass instead of making it a living, breathing vehicle that delivers an abundant life as you enjoy God's promises for you.

Today, religions ask you to sign on to the traditions and rules ... but deny you any possibility of relationship with God, unless you have a higher than passing grade on their "performance" oriented scorecard.

Religion of man or Relationship with God? You must choose. It's your eternity, and just as important, it's your life in route to that eternity.

The good news I'll share with you in this book is that if you accept God's free gift of Relationship based on what He provided for you through the work of Jesus, and not allow any religious opinion to corrupt or contaminate that relationship, you'll find a way to make your church experience come alive. And more importantly, you'll come alive!

Look around you. Examine your religious experience and ask the tough question: Have I found a loving, intimate relationship with God?

Unfortunately, if you are seeking a personal relationship and a fruitful fellowship with God, you may instead be finding an atmosphere of guilt and shame in what many call "Traditional Churchianity".

But, you will find how to connect with God through His word.

And you will be able to do it here. Enjoy!

Randy Hammon
Laguna Niguel, CA
March 2011

Chapter 1: The God Father

Make no mistake: Religion today is getting in the way of your relationship with God.

I don't pretend that this is a simple claim to make. I understand that it is controversial. I make it all the same because I have witnessed so much of the dissatisfaction, the guilt, and the frustration that religion causes for well-intentioned people who want nothing else but to live well and to serve God.

Like Brando in the famous *Godfather* movies, God has "an offer you can't refuse" once you understand it. Yet even as we struggle to serve Him, the very religions that claim to help us are actually pushing us further from a personal, loving relationship with God the Father. To many of us, God seems distant and even frightening. Far more present in our lives are the rules and regulations of our churches—the long lists of *do dos* and *don't don'ts* that promise us heaven if we cooperate and hell if we don't.

I'm here to tell you that God doesn't have to feel so far away. I'm here to tell you that you don't need to keep constant tabs on your *do-do* and *don't-don't* list, hoping to scrape by with a passing grade. I'm here to tell you that beyond the rules, the oversight, and the traditions of man there is a vibrant, immediate, and unconditionally loving place for you.

It's called a personal relationship with God, and believe it or not, it's got nothing to do with religion.

⚬✵⚬

I'll start by telling you the story of how I came to understand the difference between religion and relationship. I don't share this story because it's particularly unique. In fact, I share it for the opposite reason. I've met so many people who have experienced the same sense of frustration with religion that

1

I did, and the same sense of joy upon finally finding a personal relationship with God. It is my hope that you, too, will recognize something of your journey in mine, and that you'll join me in walking forward towards unconditional love and grace.

My parents were not religious people, by any means. I can count on my hands the number of times they went to church during my childhood. I actually brought religion into my own life at the age of eight—because I liked the look of the Catholic school uniform. Those salt and pepper jeans and that white shirt seemed like they would make picking out an outfit for school pretty easy. Besides, all the kids in my neighborhood were attending the Catholic grammar school, and like any young boy, I wanted to be with my friends. That's how I became a Catholic—not exactly a "road to Damascus" experience!

My interest in Catholicism wasn't entirely superficial. In fact, I really took to it. I took to heart the principles, the tenets and the values, and I bought—hook, line, and sinker—the list of *do-dos* and *don't-don'ts*. I was a Catholic for seventeen years, from First Communion, Confirmation, and my formative years in Catholic elementary, through an all-boy Catholic high school, and into Jesuit education at Loyola University of Los Angeles. Until I was a young man of twenty-five years, I never thought twice about Catholicism. I believed that life in this world was a test, and passing that test meant hopefully meeting God in the afterlife. Needless to say, I did what I could to make sure I scraped by with at least a passing grade.

The trouble was that I couldn't follow all the rules perfectly. As I hit my twenties and began to mature and think for myself, I started to feel increasingly ashamed of and disappointed in myself. Most of the time, I did okay, but there were always a few *do dos* that I wasn't managing to do and a few *don't-don'ts* that I couldn't help doing. As far as I could tell from the lessons in my Catholic religious education and from the Sunday sermons, in the mortal/venial sin-scoring system, I was failing. (For you non-Catholics, mortal sins send you to hell while venial sins only make you blind in one eye. If you don't confess your BIG mortal sins to a priest before you die, you might end up roasting Friday's fish with a pitchfork).

Most of the time, I would tell myself, "Hey, I'm a religious guy. I'm doing the best I can, and I think I'm on the right path," but every now and then, I'd ask myself that age-old question: "If I die tonight, do I know where I'm going?" The answer was no.

I felt like a kid in school who studies as hard as he can for a test, and who sits over his desk sweating and trying to squeeze the answers out of his memory. When he hands in the test, he feels . . . just okay. He's not really *sure* he nailed it, and he won't really know until the next day, when the teacher hands back the graded papers. Maybe he'll get a pleasant surprise and find out he did well. Then again, maybe there will be a big, red "F" waiting for him at the top of the page.

That's how I felt about my life's existence. When it came to that ultimate final exam, that transition to the other side of the curtain called death, I didn't feel secure, deep in my being, about attaining my desired destination — Heaven.

By that time in my early 20s, I was playing professional baseball and regularly getting together with a group of other guys on the team for Bible study. I found out that I wasn't the only person with the same type of concern. Some of my friends were Catholics like me, holding their breath between confessions and hoping that their prayers were passing safely to God through the designated intermediaries between God and people — the Virgin Mary and the saints. Some of my friends were in various denominations of Christianity, telling themselves, "Well, Jesus made the ultimate sacrifice for me, so even if I can't follow all the rules, I *think* I'll be okay." Some were Jewish guys, who hoped that the annual rabbinical atonements on their behalf would keep them in the clear until the next year. There were even agnostics coming to the meetings, and ultimately they too had the same question: "I'm doing the best I can, but how can I be sure? If there is a God, will He or She let me in?"

We all agreed that living with that uncertainty, that fear and doubt, was not a fulfilling way of life.

In the midst of that confusion, at the age of twenty-five, I attended a Baptist church service that changed my life. I went with the woman I was dating at the time, who would end up becoming my first wife eighteen months later. Throughout the service, I kept hearing the words "personal relationship with God."

A personal relationship with God? That was something I knew I didn't have. I had a relationship with the Catholic Church institution, but it was unfulfilling and certainly not of the intimate, personal variety. Plus, I was taught that I wasn't even worthy enough to talk directly to God. I had to make an appointment with his mom or one of his dead subordinates!

As we drove home, I started on a rant about my confusion and angst. "How do we know for sure if we're going to heaven or hell—if we're getting things right?" What about people who have never heard of this Jesus character? What about people who haven't had a chance to learn all these rules and regulations, like my parents, my brothers and other loved ones? Why are they going to hell?" I was pouring out all my doubts and frustration. I was crying out against years of religious education and a system that didn't make any sense to me in how we were sized up for our final destinations.

Suddenly, my girlfriend turned to me and asked simply, "I don't know about all of that, but are you happy?"

I said, "What do you mean, 'Am I happy?' I'm a professional baseball player. I finished my college Business degree. I'm driving around town in a new Porsche. Yeah, I guess I'm happy."

She looked at me steadily. "No," she said. "I mean . . . are you really *happy?*"

I didn't even have to pause to think. "No."

"Why not?"

"Because I'm not the kind of person I want to be," I answered.

The moment I said it, something strange happened. To this day, I can't quite describe it in words, though it was perhaps the most real and visceral experience I've ever had. I felt an enormous, powerful spiritual presence that literally overcame me. It was an energy that just shot right through my body from the floorboard of my car. I felt it, as did she. Her eyes were wide open in amazement.

It was the presence of God's Holy Spirit. He had "come a' callin'" in answer to my honest cries.

Right there, in the car with my girlfriend, I broke down and started sobbing uncontrollably. Yeah, me, the big man on campus, the pro athlete, the self-proclaimed ladies' man, broken and letting it all out before the God I so wanted to know intimately.

I looked at my girlfriend and said, "This isn't about the kind of person I want to be. I'm unhappy because I'm not the kind of person God wants me to be."

4

That was the major turning point of my life. It was March 6th, 1977.

❦

Once I had that realization—that I wasn't the kind of man God wanted me to be—it wasn't like my whole life turned on a dime. I didn't have a drinking problem to be treated; I had never taken drugs; I wasn't gambling; I didn't have cancer. It wasn't like "my wife left me with my best friend and my dog" like in a country western song. My life was functional; it just wasn't fulfilling.

The major change came from realizing that I felt unfulfilled because I had been evaluating myself from my own frame of reference instead of from God's. I had made my salvation all about my ability or lack thereof to follow the rules of the institution of Catholicism. "Accept Christ's sacrifice on the cross and keep these rules, and maybe you'll get in." God's role in this salvation process was not in the equation.

I realized in the car that what was missing from my evaluation of myself was an understanding of God's unconditional love, regardless of my ability to keep the *do do's and don't don'ts.* It wasn't about striving to follow the rules; it was about giving myself over to God's intention for my life. I understood for the first time that He wanted me to do things His way, not so that I could tally points on the *do do* and *don't don't* list, but because He just loved me and wanted me free of the religious precepts that kept me from enjoying an intimate daddy-child relationship.

This is a tough concept for us to allow into our hearts. We live in a world that falls woefully short in terms of the amount of unconditional love that goes around. Most relationships we participate in today are conditional. "You do this for me, and I'll do this for you in return." This happens in boss/employee relationships, husband/wife relationships, dating relationships, even in friendships. We give to each other because we get something in return.

Very rarely do we see, right here in this world, earthly examples of unconditional love. I'm talking about the kind of love that might lead my wife or my children or my friends to say to me, "You know what, Randy, you're a horse's ass at times, but I love you anyway." I think that's how each of us, deep down, wants to be loved by the people who are important to us. Even if we don't have that in our personal lives, that's how each one of us is loved by God.

We need that kind of love from Him, because the truth is that each of us is a horse's ass in our own way. There's not a single one of us on earth who is worthy before God to do anything of significance without His aid. We're hell-bent on doing things our way, from our perspective, in our own time, but the truth is that we can't accomplish a thing without God. We only become worthy of His love when He says to us, "Your deeds do not make you worthy of My love. I loved you first by creating you and allowing you to freely choose to accept My love. You are worthy of a relationship as My kid if you'll just accept that free gift, and forsake your efforts to earn my love. Relax, it's there for the taking!"

That's what it means to have a true, vibrant, and interactive relationship with God. He initiates love and we respond by welcoming Him into our life as our dad, our provision, and our friend. What a concept!

Unfortunately, more often than not, religion gets in the way of our submission to that. Religion, when it becomes more about fulfilling the traditions of man than about opening ourselves to God's love, is just a way for us to show God that we've earned whatever it is that we want from Him, whether it's happiness in this life or an eternity in the next.

If religion is about trying to appease God, relationship is about relinquishing ourselves to the fact that there's no reason to appease God. We can't do *anything*—not a thing—without Him. We truly have relationship with God when we stop trying to get all these rules right and instead we hear Him when he reaches down to us and says, "You can't do it. Your money's no good here! Just accept that I paid the price to the devil to buy you back from the disillusionment and emptiness that resulted from mankind demanding in the Garden of Eden[139] to do it your own way. You don't have to live under that tyrant anymore."

When we don't hear that message from God, and instead we just keep hammering away at the rules and trying to get it right without Him, all the while sinking deeper and deeper into a sense of unworthiness, that's when we're truly isolated from God. That's how religion stands in the way of relationship. That's how religion keeps us from knowing God's love.

When we accept the redemptive work of God's Messiah as promised by His prophets in the Jewish scriptures, we gain Relationship with God.

When we try to earn that relationship with our best efforts that always fall short of perfection, we gain religious frustration and futility.

Imagine a relationship between a parent and a child where the child feels that he has to earn his parent's love. Perhaps the parent never expected to have perfect behavior from the child, but for whatever reason, the child feels like he's letting his parent down if he doesn't have the best grades, if he doesn't make the team, if he doesn't show model behavior—if he isn't *perfect* in every way. If that child feels like he isn't getting the full, unconditional, loving relationship with his parent because he just can't measure up, how can he enjoy the journey of childhood?

This is what I came to understand that Easter when I realized that I wasn't the kind of man God wanted me to be. God wanted me to do things His way, in the same way that the loving father of a child wants to see that child get the best results from life. But whatever choices the child makes, his father loves him.

We hear the phrase "God the Father" all the time, but we don't always pause to consider what this means. In a world where we have to earn so many of our rewards, where we can't always hope to be loved unconditionally, we can turn to the God-Father for true parenting.

Even though I first began to understand the concept of God's fatherly love in 1977, it wasn't until six years later, when I became a father myself, that the knowledge really hit home. My first son Brandon was born in 1983, and he was followed by Nolan in 1985 and Dillon two years after that. They are the ones who the God-Father used through the parenting process to teach me what this whole deal called "unconditional love" is all about.

All I had to do was look for the first time at those kids to realize that, from the moment of their births until my last breath on this earth, there was nothing that any one of them was ever going to do that would make me stop loving them. Absolutely nothing. I can certainly be angry with them; I can even be disappointed in them, but they are my children. I will never stop loving them.

Unfortunately, the overwhelming majority of people in our world, whether they are Christian or Jewish or Muslim or any other religion, never get to experience the love of God as a father. When you've had a hell of a time relating to your human father or stepfather or other male influential figures in your life, how can you then relate to and understand the love of the God-Father? So often, I've heard, "God is my father? Well, if He's anything like my actual father, then I'm in big trouble."

This is the major key to why so many people in our world are frightened and miserable and searching for things like drugs, alcohol, and sex to fill the gaps left in their lives by unfulfilling relationships. When you have never experienced or never come to understand unconditional love, you are left with a lot of emptiness and unworthiness.

Jesus told us, if you want to sum it all up, "I want you to love God the best you can, and I want you to love each other as you want to be loved. If you do that, you will have fulfilled all of the Law and the teachings of the Prophets of the Jewish scriptures." This imperative appears in some form in every single one of the world's religions. Some call it the Golden Rule. We've broken it down into a list of smaller rules, from not committing murder to not stealing a soda from the grocery store, but the key element is the positive "ACTION" in loving others as you want to be loved, not "REFRAINING" from offensive behavior without doing the love "ACTION".

The fact is that we wouldn't need those rules if parents loved their children unconditionally and let them know it. If parents modeled the Golden Rule of Jesus before their kids, there would be no war, there would be no oppression and there would be no violence or sexual predation. You could go right down the list and nix them all if we strove to parent on earth the way that God parents us. I don't mean dote on your children; I don't mean coddle them; I don't mean baby them. Love them with a spirit of respect and openness. When you must discipline them, do so because you love them, and like the God-Father, tell them so.

Imperfect as my father was when it came to guiding me in matters of relating to God, he did model one thing for me: unconditional love. His motto was, "Son, I'm not going to tell you what to do, but whatever you choose, do your best, and I approve of it." This is the same attitude I have tried to pass on to my sons. There's nothing they have to do to earn it. I love them the way they are, even when they didn't want to play baseball! I'm a professional baseball player with three sons, and not one of them played baseball. I love them not in spite of it, but *for* it. I love them for who they are.

I certainly can't say that I am anywhere close to a perfect father, but I do know that my three boys and my stepson always know the one thing that is most important: their dad will always love them and absolutely accept them regardless of their behavior, choices and, yes, mistakes. Their actions may cause a disruption of our fellowship (how we function with each other), but never our relationship (who we are to each other).

They can make their own way through life, and they can make mistakes, but they know that if they do make a mistake, they can come back to me, and they aren't going to hear, "I told you so." The fact is that nobody ever has to tell you, "I told you so"—you'll be the first one to tell yourself that when you make a mistake. That's how I helped my boys come to understand that no one is ever going to find peace as an island, trying to do everything alone without God's participation as the God-Father.

This is how God loves us. I was lucky because I had a model of this type of love in my own father, and so it was something I was able to understand. It readied me to crave a personal relationship with God as my father. I was ready to talk with Him and be taught by Him. I was ready to find the peace of mind and contentment that can only come with a personal relationship.

Just as my boys learned growing up, I know that I can do things the wrong way. I can sin; I can have an affair; I can cheat people in business. I can do any one of those things because I am a flesh and blood man. I am a carnal man. And knowing that I *can* do those things, I don't have any desire to do them.

I know I'm free to live outside God's love and to shun His way. I know I'm free to mess up and then to turn around and say, "Oh, jeez, I'm sorry." But knowing that I'm truly loved by God completely obliterates all the stupid reasons why I might violate my relationship with Him and my relationships with my family. I could . . . but I don't need to. I care too much about our Relationship.

That is why I'm writing this book. When you're following the rules to earn admission to heaven because religion tells you to, it's easy to slip up. It's easy to make mistakes and to hurt people, and not to grow from those experiences that cause unending guilt, remorse and hopelessness, but when you're living well and loving God and others because you want to honor your *relationships*, it's suddenly very simple. You no longer have to police yourself without being certain of the pay-off. You no longer have to play God.

Religion without a father-child relationship with God is a complete waste of time because man's effort to appease God instead of responding to God's desire for Relationship is a complete waste of time. All God asks of us is that we love Him and be in relationship with Him. If He wanted a family that simply followed the list of *do dos* and *don't don'ts*, He would have created a world populated with billions of robots.

Instead He gave us the ability to choose how we behave. He gave us the ability to shun Him or to accept that there is a God who loves us, who creates order, who wants Fellowship, and who wants us to love Him not because we must but because we want to.

If we choose not to love Him, he'll continue to love us. It will never be too late for us to come back to Him and say, "All right. I screwed up. But what now? What's the right thing for me to do, from *this* point forward?"

The right thing to do is to create the relationship that you have always prayed for, that you have always longed to have with God, but that you have yet to experience because all those rules got in the way. In this book, together, we'll find a path to doing just that—to forgetting what was wrong, and deciding to focus on the future with our God-Father.

For those of you who don't believe in God, my request of you would be to honestly answer this question: would you like there to be a loving God-Father? A dad who desires a loving Relationship with you regardless of the insufficient, misguided or misplaced love you got from your earthly parents.

Come on! If you're just heading for the transition into "nothingness" at the end of life's road anyway, why not humor me for a few more pages to explore what "could be."

God dares you!

CHAPTER 2: THE DEVIL'S WAR

I've always enjoyed a good epic. Whether it's the *Star Wars* movies, *The Matrix*, or the *Lord of the Rings* trilogy—which my sons got me into—there's something powerful about good versus evil. People like a hero who must overcome great challenges and adversity. As far as I know, smooth sailing never brought forth a good story.

It's in our nature to love epics. Why? Because each of us is living one.

About ten years ago, I read a book called *Epic: The Story God is Telling* by John Eldredge. After he published *Wild at Heart*, Eldredge wrote this book about all the great epic stories in the Bible: David and Goliath, Moses leading his people out of Egypt, Daniel being thrown into the lion's den, etc. As I was reading *Epic*, I began to understand for the first time that our life is yet another great epic and, like any epic, there is a battle.

When I say "life is a battle," I don't mean it metaphorically. Yes, life is hard, and sometimes it feels like we spend each day fighting–with our spouses, with our boss, with the rush hour traffic–but the warfare I'm talking about is not theoretical or implied. It's very real, and it's happening every day of our lives, whether we're aware of it or not. We are living amidst a spiritual war, and it's a life or death situation.

Every time we face an obstacle, we ask the question, "Why?" If we lose our job or someone close to us passes away, we want to know where these obstacles are coming from. I'll tell you where they're coming from: the devil.

The devil goes by many names—Lucifer, Satan, the beast. Like in any epic, he represents the forces of evil. But the devil is far more powerful than Darth Vader or Lord Sauron. He's a gifted deceiver and a consummate shape-shifter. When Satan revealed himself to man and woman in the Garden of Eden, he came as a serpent. He whispered to Adam and Eve to eat the fruit from the forbidden tree—to do it their way instead of God's way–and they listened.

Mankind has been trying to do the same thing ever since. Both in churches and out of them, from humanism to communism, man is bent on doing it his way, but if we are honest with ourselves, we can't help but wonder why we get mercilessly buffeted and beat up in the process. Our lives are a constant battle to do what we want to do, but we're constantly coming up against obstacles. We face financial challenges, marital strife, illness, tension in relationships, loss, and general evil in the world.

Some men and women face these battles and fight bravely, but many more give up. They turn to alcohol and drugs, trying to numb out the pain. They acquiesce to temptation and compromise their integrity. There are very few people who, at the end of their lives, can say, "I fought the good fight. I have done what I intended to do." And yet that is exactly the kind of person God calls us to be.

I believe we have real foes. There are spiritual beings at war all around us— angels versus demons, and the devil versus all of us. Our battle is not against flesh and blood; it's against principalities and powers and angelic beings who have rebelled against God. Satan himself is a fallen angel; he tried to unseat God and was cast out of heaven. I've battled these forces in my own life, arming myself with Scripture and prayer, and God has advised my spirit.

In 2 Kings 6:8-23, the Bible tells the following story. Elisha, the prophet, warned the King of Israel that his enemies were planning an attack. The King of Aram was furious that Elisha was able to predict his every move, so he sent an army of men by nightfall to surround the city and capture the prophet.

When Elisha's servant arose the following morning and went outside, he saw the army surrounding the city. "Oh, my lord," he asked his master. "What shall we do?"

"Don't be afraid," the prophet answered. "Those who are with us are more than those who are with them." Then Elisha prayed to God, "O Lord, open his eyes so he may see."

The Lord opened the servant's eyes, and when he did, he was able to see the hills full of horses and chariots of fire all around Elisha. There were thousands of angelic beings that had surrounded the city, unbeknownst to the enemy. Then Elisha prayed that God would strike the enemy with blindness. The army fell into such mass confusion that Elisha was able to lead them directly to the King of Israel.

The epic stories of the Old Testament aren't fantasy. God hasn't given us fairy tales to fight real-world battles. Instead, he has given us real-world weapons. But first we have to understand that there is a battle, and why God allows it to be so.

⚜

How many times in your life have you asked the following question: "Why did God allow this to happen?" We want to know why He didn't prevent a disaster or tragedy—why He lets bad things happen to good people. Why did God allow the earthquake in Haiti? Why has He allowed genocide in Darfur? Recently I even heard someone ask why God allowed the oil spill in the Gulf Coast!

Unless I missed that part of Scripture, I don't remember God Enterprises investing in BP and digging that well. I'm sad to say, these questions are keeping people from God because they're skewing what's really going on. It all has to do with free will.

Like any great general, God has already made the vision for the battle. He's got a masterful battle plan, but because he created us with free will, *we get to make a choice.* God created a world where we can choose right and wrong, and when people choose wrong, we suffer. Because of man's choices not to abide by the Golden Rule—to love God with everything we've got and to love others the way we want to be loved—the world is in chaos. Mankind has been listening to the wrong voice—the voice of the enemy. It is this voice that appeals to human greed, jealousy, and arrogance. The struggles in our life are not reason to reject God—on the contrary. They are the heartbreaking results of a rejection of God that has been ongoing since the Fall of Man.

Everything on earth, from the animals to the vegetation to the weather systems, was made for man to enjoy. Man himself was made because God desired fellowship. He created man because He desired a relationship with him.

We all enjoy fellowship when it's not forced. I courted my wife and we got to know each other in depth before I asked her to marry me; I didn't buy a girl from the Eastern block, bring her back to the States, and force her to be my wife. Of the two, which relationship do you think is the deepest and most enjoyable?

Our relationship with God works the same way. God doesn't force man to love Him. He loved us enough to give us free will, and it's up to us how we respond. With freedom comes the possibility of rebellion, and our sin nature is constantly tempting us to rebel. That's where the war takes place—in our rebellion.

The enemy gains a foothold into our lives in two places. The first place is in preventing the initial relationship. Satan would be happy if no one trusted in Christ; it's his desire to prevent people from coming to know God by keeping us from accepting Jesus as our personal savior. As believers, we've won that battle. We have eternal life in his Son.

The battle doesn't stop there. Once you're in a relationship with God, the warfare continues. Satan is dead-set on disrupting and destroying your relationship, making it ineffective in whatever way possible. It's the same thing that happens in our relationships with our spouses, our kids, and our co-workers. It's a constant battle to keep our personal relationships loving and productive.

Satan preys on relationships. He sows seeds of discord in our hearts and we begin to question them. "Am I getting an equal amount out of this relationship?" we say. "Seems like it's all going out and not coming in." Temptation comes in many forms, and when it comes to our relationship with God, the devil attacks the area where we are most vulnerable: our uncertainty.

Our culture is very metaphysical. One of the most popular books ever written is *Think and Grow Rich* by Napoleon Hill. First published in 1937, it's still a perennial bestseller after seventy years. I've yet to meet a businessperson who hasn't read it. Hill's methodology is constructed around his communion with "spirit guides"— great men of the past like Abraham Lincoln and Andrew Carnegie. Hill claims that these leaders gave him the truth about how to be successful and grow mighty empires.

The fact that this book has been a bestseller for nearly a century tells me something about our culture. We're longing to believe in the supernatural. You've also got all the people who believe in reincarnation and you've got the psychics and the astrologers who defer to the Zodiac to plan out their future, from where they should live to whom they should marry. Sylvia Browne is America's most famous psychic. She's written fifty-seven books, and every one of them has hit bestseller status. She's almost as popular as Oprah!

You might be saying, "That's just entertainment." But is it? To me, it's obvious that people are searching for metaphysical significance. We're drawn to it, like a moth to a flame. Yet people roll their eyes at the idea of "extraterrestrial" angelic and demonic beings. The world is fascinated by the spiritual world; it's just not fascinated by the spiritual world of God!

People are searching for the supernatural, but they're missing the truth that's right in front of them–the existence of a just and loving God who wants a personal relationship with us, his children. In our fallen world, people are turning farther and farther from their God-Father. The atheists believe that there is no God, that we just crawled out of the muddy banks of the primordial ooze, and that there's no rhyme or reason to our lives. There's a semblance of right and wrong, but there are no angels, no devils, no God— nothing. Just us. We roll down the highway of our lives with no greater purpose, no belief in something more, and at the end we die. Sadly, we're perpetuating this nothingness into the next generation. I see evidence of nihilism everywhere I look.

There's another highway—a far better one. As the great philosopher Blaise Pascal said, "There is a God-shaped vacuum in the heart of every man which cannot be filled by any created thing, but only by God, the Creator, made known through Jesus." Each of us has a vacuum in our spirit that cries out to be filled by something larger than ourselves. We crave it. From day one of creation up to this moment right now, we have been trying to fill that vacuum with anything and everything we can get our hands on—drugs, alcohol, success, love—when in reality, the only thing that fits into that space is God.

From the early days of polytheism when the Mayans worshipped their gods, through the rising popularity of atheism tied to Marxism in the 1800s, human beings have been aware of this vacuum. It just feels right to believe in someone bigger than ourselves. The celestial stars are one of my favorite proofs of the existence of an almighty God. I look up into the night sky and try to imagine what's beyond it—beyond the clouds, beyond the earth's stratosphere, beyond the crescent-shaped universe. That's the greatest example of eternity I could ever imagine.

The reason I wrote this book is to underline the divide between religion and a personal relationship with Christ. The church could and should be the place where we learn the truth about the spiritual warfare we're living in. Instead, the church has succumbed to the enemy in the form of fear.

Fear is pervasive in our culture. People are scared to death that they're going to have to live eternally with the same doubt, confusion, and apathy that they're living in this life devoid of God. Life without God is meaningless. It's devoid of purpose because there is no understanding that God put us here, in the middle of an epic, to fight a spiritual battle. As Christians, knowing this gives us hope, and by definition, hope is *future*. If we come to the end of the road and there's nothing on the other side, we're screwed.

It is this pervasive fear which has infiltrated our churches and rendered them ineffective today. A number of Christian leaders don't want to entertain the fact that there's a war going on. They feel frustrated, limited, and inefficient, and they're downright scared to death of awakening something as vast and serious as spiritual warfare, so they kind of let sleeping dogs lie. They adopt a strategy of avoidance. Just ignore what's going on around you and you'll be fine.

We won't be fine. We are under attack from every direction. The church has failed us by not helping us understand the players in the battle. The head players are, of course, God and His arch-enemy Satan. Think of them like two coaches leading opposing teams. Then there are sub-coaches and players, lieutenants and privates who are working for the big guys. These are the angels and demons. The demonic beings are Satan's right-hand men, and they never rest in their attempt to lure believers off-track.

I don't think the church is intentionally getting it wrong. They're not trying to screw things up or lead us astray, but sometimes they face restrictions on what they can say. I can share these stories because I'm not paid by a religious organization. My life is not going to economically fall apart if I challenge you to accept that we are living amidst a war, but for most Christian leaders, there's an awful lot at stake. When they receive revelation, when their eyes get opened by the truth that is in God's word, the demands can be too much. "I'm not doing that," they say. "I can't share that with my congregation." To do so would take a tremendous amount of courage, because it could very well cost them their job or economic well-being.

Whenever a discussion of spiritual warfare is brought up, Satan is right there, immediately trying to distract us. Our minds become cluttered by doubt and confusion. We're a muddled mess. Satan uses the distractions in our own lives to pull our focus away from the important stuff. We become caught up in issues in our marriages, with our kids, and in our businesses. We're consumed by health problems or tension with friends. These are the weapons that the enemy uses to distract us from the vision that God has created.

We are constantly under attack by the devil and his minions. That's why we have to fight for our kingdom. My kingdom is my family—my wife and my kids—and my position in the community and at work. I am the king of the domain God has given me. I respect it, I honor it, and I fight for it. If somebody tries to break into my house, they're going to pay the price. If they try to attack my wife or hurt my kids, they're going to pay the price. I know my authority.

God's desire is that, like any good soldier, we know our authority and are trained in the right weapons to assert that authority. The right weapons are the key to maintaining that which you have, have fought for, and currently possess.

The majority of people don't know there's a war going on. Churches aren't talking about it—it's a touchy subject, good and evil—but we have to understand that there is a battleground. The battleground is not the physical earth itself; it is the people who inhabit it. The battleground is us. God is not concerned about establishing a relationship with planet Earth or the cosmos. He is concerned about having people understand His love. He is interested in redeeming His relationship with us, His children, so that He can train us to fight and win the battle.

Why is it that we can understand the concept of competition everywhere but our spiritual lives? You can bet John D. Rockefeller understood the idea of warfare in business—he crushed the competition to become a titan of industry. There's the same sense of cutthroat competition on the spiritual plane. The devil and his servants are vying with God for power over you. The enemy wants to try and steal your joy, your family, and your possessions. He is attacking us every day, and still our churches remain silent on the subject.

Satan is well-equipped for battle. We're all familiar with the weapons of warfare that he uses against us: jealousy, hatred, covetousness. We can go down the list: deceit, depression, addiction. Have you ever wondered why they call alcohol "spirits"? I have seen alcohol influence people so strongly that they want to commit suicide. Their chronic intoxication becomes like a demon, completely changing who they are. I've engaged in spiritual warfare when people were so drunk that they actually tried to kill themselves.

I'm just a man who loves God. I'm no hero, but I am a spiritual warrior, if only because the Lord requires me to be so. I read the Bible daily and have absorbed the weapons of warfare God promises his children. They're not physical; they're spiritual. "Put on the full armor of God," says Ephesians 6:11, "so that you can take your stand against the devil's schemes." The armor of God includes the belt of truth, the breastplate of righteousness, the helmet of salvation, the shield of faith, and the sword of the Spirit, which is the word of God.

This is battle language. We're not talking about a silly costume; we're talking about the clothes of a great warrior. The shield of faith represents action. Faith is not a belief system; it's trying to actively follow God's word. Most of the battle attire is defensive; clothe yourself in these garments, and the Lord will protect you from attack. There's only one offensive weapon in the whole armor, and it's the sword of the Spirit. If you take on this weaponry, you will emerge victorious from the battlefield of life.

⚜

The story of Abraham and Isaac is one of my favorites. God instructed Abraham to take his beloved son Isaac up on the mount and sacrifice him. Now, I guarantee you that would flip out 95 percent of Christians today. "God wants me to what? Kill my son?"

Here's the thing. When Abraham took his servants to the mountain, he gave them very specific instructions. "Stay here with the donkey while I and the boy go over there," he says in Genesis 22:5. "We will worship and then we will come back to you."

That passage of Scripture blows me away. Abraham had such confidence in God that, although he knew why he was going up to the mountain, he fully expected to come back down with his son unharmed. Sure enough, as Abraham was about to sacrifice his own son, God saw that his heart was right.

18

"Do not lay a hand on the boy," said the Lord. "Do not do anything to him; for now I know that you fear God, because you have not withheld from me your son, your only son."

Abraham looked up and saw a ram caught by its horns, and this became the sacrifice. Just as Abraham had said to his servants, he and his son returned safely back to them.

As Christians, we have the same symbolism. God did not withhold from us His only son; He sacrificed Him so that we might have eternal life. Why? Because "God so loved the world that He gave His only begotten son." He loved us. He has always loved us, and He loves us still.

God wants communion and fellowship with us. He wants us to come directly to Him so that He can arm us to fight the battle of a lifetime. It's just like how we as parents want our kids to come to us when they're having a problem at school or they need help. As I raise my sons, I tell them not to be shy. This is a battlefield, but there's no need to be afraid of it.

Issues are going to come up for our kids; maybe they'll be offered drugs or be tempted by premarital sex. All of this is part of the warfare. Simply be aware that it could happen. It's like soldiers in a platoon. The general tells them that there are landmines in the field of duty, just like God warns us of the traps the devil has laid. Don't be afraid, just let the Lord train you to deal with it.

The closer our walk with God, the more weapons we have at our disposal. In my own walk, these weapons are usually what God has said about something—a potent piece of Scripture or the Lord speaking to me in my prayer life. I arm myself with God's wisdom in Proverbs and God's love in Psalms. The stories of David and Joseph give me hope and inspiration, reinvigorating my faith. Through daily fellowship and reading His word, God prepares me for the epic of my life.

Philippians 4:13 says, "I can do all things through Christ who strengthens me." We can do diddly-squat on our own. We aren't that smart. We aren't that righteous. We aren't that talented. But when we are empowered by the spirit of God, we can be like Moses leading his people out of Egypt or Joseph rising to be the Pharaoh's second-in-command after years of slavery and imprisonment.

If we have the right weapons, we'll win the battle, but if we walk out there without any armor and start throwing punches against guys who have machine guns, we're going to lose. The only way we can acquire the right weapons and training for battle is through the Spirit of God.

I believe heartily in the protection and provisions of God. If God didn't give mankind the ability to fight these spiritual battles, we'd be helpless. [108] But He did give use everything we need in his Son. When we pray and acknowledge to God that He is God our Savior, He will equip us in the armor of the Lord. We will charge forward toward hope, not nothingness.

The church misses it because they don't realize that we're in the kingdom of God now. It's not something we're going to get on the other side of the curtain. We're living in it right now. We have a war to be fought to preserve the kingdom we're given—our families, our earthly domain—and the kingdom of our relationship with God.

You might say we're in training for something we don't entirely understand. The spiritual warfare is beyond our comprehension as mortals, but God is training us in this life to exercise faith, which is action on His word. You can't step out in ignorance—you'll hit a landmine—but if you educate and prepare yourself, utilizing what God has given you in your study of Scripture and your personal relationship with Him, you will be armed for battle.

Are you prepared for the epic of your life? God yearns to have you in His army as an impassioned, empowered warrior for Christ. Will you heed the call?

CHAPTER 3: GROW YOUR RELATIONSHIPS, NOT YOUR OBLIGATIONS

God's word never says that you have to do certain things, other than accept what he has done for you, in order for you to have a relationship with God. Contrary to what the traditions of men might say, your ability to join into relationship with God is not predicated upon obligations on your part.

When we look at Jewish tradition, we see that Jews have an understanding that laws exist in order to help them function with each other and to function in a relationship with God. But adherence to these laws is not an obligation that establishes a relationship with God. In Jewish tradition, the High Priest goes to the Holy of Holies to sprinkle the blood of the sacrificial lamb, and the people have to look upon that sacrifice and accept it as a symbol of their atonement so they can freely accept a relationship with God. Their only obligation is one of acceptance.

Since acceptance of God's sacrifice is our only obligation to God, let's discuss how we can focus on and grow our relationships instead of our obligations.

Let's start with your relationship with God. If you ask, "What obligation is necessary to grow my relationship with God?" the traditions of men will hand you as many obligations as there are religions out there. There are countless denominations in the Christian faith, and even in the Jewish and Muslim faiths—Orthodox segments all the way down to liberal ones. The traditions of men will always have an answer for what obligations are necessary to please God.

In the first chapter of this book, "The God Father," I talked about the fact that God expects nothing other than obedience. In fact, the Bible tells the story of Samuel, a prophet who told Saul, "To obey is better than to sacrifice." In that story, God ordered Saul to destroy a particular city, Amalek, because the

Amalekites were in complete disobedience to God's laws and were trying to destroy the nation of Israel. If the nation of Israel were destroyed, then the Messiah would never come forward.

Over the years, God supernaturally preserved the leaders of the nation of Israel, from Noah to Moses to Isaac to Jacob, and so forth. God miraculously protected them to preserve the righteous bloodline so that the Messiah would come through the twelve tribes of Israel—specifically through Judah.

When God ordered Saul, the king of Israel, to take down the Amalekites, God specifically instructed him to destroy everyone and everything, but Saul brought the king back alive and kept some of the animals alive. Samuel approached Saul the next morning and said, "What are those animals I hear? You were supposed to destroy everything."

This act of disobedience marks the turning point at which God took the kingdom of Israel away from Saul and imparted it to David. Through the prophet Samuel, God said, "To obey is better than to sacrifice." That phrase, in a nutshell, shows how our relationship with God is established, and also how it flourishes. Obedience is the key to that relationship.

So what is obedience? We're not talking about obedience to the law or to rules, but about obedience to God—the acceptance of God's gift of relationship. God uses the story of Saul to zero in on this irrefutable principle of obedience. God is more concerned with us obeying Him than He is with us adhering to the traditions of men.

Saul, who was engrossed in the traditions of men, thought to himself, "I know God said this, but I'm going to do this instead because I'm sure God will be pleased to see that I've got this king on a rope and I've got these animals and spoils. Praise be to God." God looked at the goods and said, "Is that what I told you to do?"

God says the same thing today. God doesn't concern himself with how much money you make, how much money you give, or what charities you give to. God doesn't look at the number of people you welcome into your home or the number of people you kill in war. He asks you to do one thing: to establish Relationship with Him. This is obedience. To accept what *God* did so that you can receive salvation. After you accept that, *then* God talks to you about the requirements of maintaining a functional fellowship with him.

God essentially said to Saul, "You disobeyed me." God didn't say, "You didn't perform for me." He said, "You disobeyed me."

What do religions and the traditions of men constantly hammer into us? Performance. Sacrifice. They give us the mindset of Saul, who thought, "But I performed for you," but God, first and foremost, wants to establish a relationship with you, and that relationship can't be earned by anything you do.

God knew that we're not able to enter freely into Relationship with Him without His help. Mankind is stuck in Satan's prison, and because we're in that prison, we can't let ourselves out. Only God can do that. So God came to earth, partook in our human nature in the form of Jesus Christ, and functioned as a man with divine thoughts and divine powers. He felt as a man, loved as a man, and existed to demonstrate true obedience to God so that we could see what a proper, functional fellowship with God looks like. God did all the work through Jesus, and all he wants us to do is accept what he did to let us out of our prison so that we can have a relationship with Him. Anything outside of this concept is what we call the law—the *do-dos* and *don't-don'ts*.

God's Bible gives us the precepts for what to do and not to do to maintain and prosper our fellowship with God. But those *do-dos* and *don't-don'ts* are not what *establish* our relationship with Him. The basis of Christianity is that Jesus came so that we wouldn't have to *do* anything to reach God.

There are plenty of scriptures that say that the coming of the Messiah will be a real eye-opening revelation for everyone. Whether that means Jesus will return or the Messiah the Jews are waiting for will come is a difference of opinion, but both groups are waiting for this messiah, and eyes will be opened one way or the other.

The premise of God's first relationship with us is established through our obedience to his word. We can apply this principle to our relationships with each other. A true love relationship is established freely between two people, and *after* they establish that relationship freely by accepting their love for each other, certain obligations appear later in order to keep their fellowship fruitful and functional.

While this mutual love relationship is ideal, there are plenty of examples in the Bible that show how God uses bizarre, dysfunctional families to fulfill His plans. Even today, arranged marriages exist and there are women who are obligated by their law, their religion, or their family to marry a certain person, but this doesn't mean that God can't use this kind of union to bless people.

Let's go to Jacob's story as an example. Jacob goes to Uncle Laban, who has two daughters, Rachel and Leah. Jacob wants to marry Rachel, the more beautiful of the two, and works for Laban for seven years in exchange for her hand in marriage. Laban tricks Jacob, marries him to Leah instead, and Jacob works another seven years before he can also marry Rachel. Eventually, Jacob also sleeps with his wives' handmaidens, and from the sons of those four women, God establishes the twelve tribes of Israel.

If God can take *that* chaos and turn it into the bloodline through which he performs his miracles and brings forth the Messiah, God can choose to take any broken family and do the same.

Today, we get so caught up in the traditions of men and what certain religions might say about divorce being the unpardonable sin that we fixate on our dysfunctional lives and believe that God can't use us to do great things anymore. That's simply untrue.

We need to remember that in relationships, Jesus' bottom line can be summarized by the golden rule: love others as you want to be loved.

I wouldn't want my wife Crystal to have an affair, so I'm not going to have an affair either. That's not how I want to be loved, and I can use that as a framework for knowing that's probably not the way she wants to be loved. I'm not going to physically or verbally berate her or abuse her because I wouldn't want that. I'm not going to cheat her financially because I wouldn't want that. When you truly function well in love by loving as you want to be loved and giving as you would like people to give to you, then although you are completely free to abuse that relationship, you choose not to because you don't want to.

Just as you are free to abuse that relationship, you are also free to obey and remain in love. That's the paradox: you're free to obey. You might argue that this, by its very definition, means that you're not free, but no. This means you are free to look at God, at yourself, at the people you love, and at the traditions of men and make your own decision regarding where you want to go. That's freedom.

While this may still seem like a paradox, it's important to remember that our walk with God is a paradox. As Jesus said, if you want to be first, you've got to be last. If you want to be served, become a servant. If you want to receive, give. If you want to live, you have to die to yourself and to your own selfish ambition and selfish understanding. Saul didn't understand this. He yielded to his selfish ambition and selfish understanding, and as a result, he lost his freedom. He lost his place as king.

A verse I will bring up throughout this book is in Numbers 23, which says, "God is not a man, that he should lie, nor a son of man, that he should change his mind. Does he speak and then not act? Does he promise and not fulfill?" This verse says that whatever God speaks will come to pass. If you make that scripture your mantra for how you deal with and function in your relationship with God, you will be able to take Him at His word and you will expect nothing short of what He has said in the word He has for you. In any situation, in any relationship or in any business transaction, your only obligation is to take God at His word. Just as you accept His free gift of relationship and salvation, you have to accept what God says about everything else and rely on that word to stay the course.

What does it mean to "stay the course"?

In the story of David, who takes over Saul's position as king of Israel, Samuel the prophet approaches Jesse, David's dad, and tells him, "Among your sons is the future king of Israel, and I'm here to anoint him." Jesse brings all his sons except for David to Samuel, and the Holy Spirit tells Samuel, "He's not here."

When Samuel asks Jesse if anybody is missing, Jesse says, "Yeah, the youngest is out in the field, taking care of business. Certainly he can't be the one you're looking for." But David was exactly who God was looking for. Saul was Israel's idea of a king, but he turned out to be a selfish, self-absorbed ruler. God's choice was David, who was an unassuming shepherd whose dad didn't even think he was fit to be a king.

Samuel anointed David as the future king, but what were his next few years like after that anointing? Complete chaos. After Samuel anointed David, he had his victory over Goliath and several other victories as one of Saul's great military leaders, but Saul was so jealous of him that David was on the run for several years because Saul wanted to kill him.

From a human perspective, everything that happened between David's anointing and him actually becoming king at age 40 appears to be in complete contradiction of God's word regarding his life.

God allows these contradictions to test our faith and our ability to stick to the course laid out before us. That faith can only come from an adherence to God's word. As Numbers 23 says, God is not a liar. God fulfills his word, and God tests us to find out whether we believe that.

We can study the biographies of any great man of God and see that this is true. Joseph, for example, dreams that his brothers and parents will bow to him, but once he exposes this dream to them, they throw him in a pit and he's sold into slavery in Egypt. When God elevates him to the position of a butler and he runs the household of one of Pharaoh's great captains, Potiphar, Potiphar's wife throws herself at Joseph. Joseph hesitates, but he remains obedient to his duties and says, "I'm not going to do this. I'm not going to dishonor my lord, Potiphar." What happens when Joseph does the right thing? Potiphar's wife grabs his robe, and as he runs away naked, she yells rape and he gets thrown in prison for many years.

God told Joseph that he would end up in a position of importance in God's kingdom, but he ends up in prison. Something about that situation doesn't add up. Joseph could easily say that God is a liar.

While Joseph is in prison, he sees the distraught countenances of a baker and a butler who are also in prison due to misunderstandings. When Joseph asks them what's wrong, they tell him about their dreams. Joseph says, "Hey! That's my expertise! Dreams are what I'm made of," and interprets their dreams for them.

The butler and baker eventually leave prison, and in the meantime Joseph takes on roles of authority in the prison, which we can see is God preparing him to rule and administer the people God will bring to him in the future.

One day, when Pharaoh has a dream that requires interpretation, the butler and the baker remember Joseph and suggest his services to Pharaoh. Pharaoh calls for Joseph and Joseph interprets the dream, which predicts seven prosperous years in Egypt followed by seven years of horrendous famine. Pharaoh then puts Joseph in charge of the entire economy of Egypt and charges him to store up grain in preparation for that famine.

When the time of famine comes, Joseph's brothers and his father, Jacob, have to go to Egypt for grain to save their family. When they do, they literally fulfill what God told Joseph years before in his dreams by approaching him and bowing down to him. The family doesn't even recognize Joseph, and in this beautiful moment, the Bible says that Joseph, overcome with emotion, excuses himself, goes behind the throne room to collect himself, then returns and reconciles with his family. This reunion is one of the most beautiful stories in the Bible.

Joseph could have been discouraged by all the hardships he experienced, but he remained obedient to God's word, survived his season of contradiction, and saved his family and the future nation of Israel.

I tell you this story to remind you that yes, God tells us what will happen in our lives. God reveals to us what will happen in our relationships at work, in our families, and in our futures, but he always tests the good revelations that we receive because God wants to build up enough character in us so that we will trust him in spite of what we sense and what we see.

Will you trust your circumstances or will you trust God?

In this book, we will address this idea of an active faith which hangs on to what God says in spite of what problems arise in our lives. When you cling to God's word, you receive the results and the fruit of that relationship with God because you have trusted Him as you fellowship with Him. Your obligation to keep the relationship going with God is obedience, not sacrifice.

Likewise, your obligation to establish a proper relationship with your wife and with your kids is obedience to God's word concerning how to function with them. It goes back to the golden rule. Love them as you want to be loved. Parent them as you wish your parents had parented you.

Even love for your family is not sacrifice. Many men believe they're being great dads because they're working 80 hours a week and traveling all over the world while not raising up their kids and not being there for their kids. They put the almighty dollar first, then say, "I have sacrificed for you. I've provided for you," but all the kids wanted was their dad, not his money. When their dad dies, the kids won't talk about the contents of their dad's will. They will talk about the ways they received fellowship and relationship with him. How do we choose that fellowship? Through obedience to God's word—the golden rule

Many religions, on the other hand, emphasize that in order to receive from God, we have to perform in certain ways and fulfill a thousand different obligations. I was raised as a Catholic, and was taught that if I wanted to knock years off of purgatory, I had to adhere to a list of *do-dos* and *don't-don'ts*. Purgatory is what the Catholics believe is a limbo existence between heaven and hell. This idea was established in the Middle Ages so that the Church could charge people financially, through indulgences, to try to secure their lot in heaven. By emphasizing that it was the people's actions that could help them reach God, the Church kept the people guessing about their salvation, which kept the money coming in. The Catholic Church, in the Middle Ages, emphasized that you had to earn your way into heaven and pay your way out of purgatory.

I was raised with this same idea that in order to please God, I needed to give Him something or do something. I was taught that if I committed a certain sin, only a certain act of confession or penance could fully allow that sin to be forgiven. What I've come to learn is that this is nowhere to be found in scripture—not in the scriptures of Israel, nor in the scriptures of the New Testament.

That tradition of men is one of the reasons that I left the Catholic Church. I was doing too much and was miserable while trying to earn God's love and salvation. I never knew whether I was headed for heaven or hell. There was no way to know whether I was making the grade. Which sin was a grievous, mortal sin? Which sin was small and deserving only of a year or so in purgatory? I lived under these questions from when I was 8 years old until I left that tradition and found a free relationship with God through Christ at age 25.

When I wrote the book *The Safe Money System*, I was sick and tired of the traditions of men on Wall Street, who laid out manmade, arbitrary rules regarding how to obtain wealth in this life. They pushed the idea of a gambling casino, but not everyone can afford to gamble!

In a way, what this book talks about is a "Safe Relationship System" with God. God doesn't need your performance. He needs only for you to have faith that what He did was enough. Once that's established, you are then free to move into a functional relationship with Him based on His word. Even then, your failure to maintain that functional relationship is not going to send you to hell. Let me say that again. God's gift of relationship with you—God's salvation for you—is free. It's done. The only requirement is your acceptance. This means that goofing up along the way in this relationship with God can't send you to hell. God took care of the salvation part. Now He just wants you to love Him with everything you've got, honor Him with everything you've got, and love your neighbor and fellow man in the same way.

God wants us to be givers. How we give is the true measure of love—how we give of our time, our money, and our resources.

One of my mentors, Mike Murdoch, says that when you're given the opportunity, don't sell your time. Sow your time.

Outside of the context of your professional work, when you come across an opportunity to help somebody, it's more valuable to sow your time because a sale is a one-time transaction, but sowing stores up the treasures of heaven. Because of your obedience in sowing of your money, your time, and your life, God will be able to have more to draw upon to bring His kingdom to earth on this side of the curtain called life.

This is the kind of wealth we should seek—God's wealth, God's provision. While it may look like you don't have a lot of money in the bank, God has a bank that can't be broken into, and the Bible says that when you come to God in faith and you seek the kingdom first, God rewards you with everything else you need as well. Jesus said that when a child comes to his father and asks for bread, his father doesn't give him a rock. Jesus said that when your child comes to you and asks for something, you, as a loving parent, will always give your child the right thing, not the wrong thing. How much more will your Father in Heaven give good things to those who love and trust Him as we are obedient in our relationship with Him?

Throughout the teachings of the Old Testament—from Proverbs to Ecclesiastes to the lives of the great prophets—we find stories of people who approach God with their needs and see God meet those needs.

Another story of obedience in relationship with God is the story of the prophet Elijah. Elijah went before Ahab, the king of Israel, and Jezebel, his heathen queen, who lured the nation of Israel into idolatrous worship of Baal. Elijah prophesied against them, and Jezebel didn't like it, so Elijah challenged the nation and its priests to a contest.

Elijah said, "Let me show you who God is. Let me show you that what I'm saying is true." So Elijah had the priests stack sacrificial animals on an altar and told them to ask their gods to pour down fire from heaven to consume those animals. Elijah said, "Certainly, your gods are powerful enough to do that."

So the priests obliged, then ranted, raved, prayed, squelched, and nothing happened. Then Elijah said, "Now if you'll get out of the way, let me show you the God—the mighty God, the king of the universe, almighty Jehovah." He said, "To show the power of God, soak the animals, build a moat around the altar, fill it with water, and get out of the way."

What I find interesting is that God not only pours fire from heaven and consumes the altar, but also consumes every one of the priests who marched around the altar and watched this happen.

This is one of the greatest exhibitions of the power of God in the Bible, which occurred because one man was obedient to the word he heard from God. However, in the next chapter, you see this same man, Elijah, running for his life because Queen Jezebel is livid because of what happened to her priests.

Elijah runs into a cave and wishes he were never born, even after he witnessed such a great act of God! This is where we find the term "the still small voice." The still small voice of the Holy Spirit speaks to Elijah and calls out his fatigue and lack of faith. He encourages Elijah by telling him that in the next town, many people who love and honor God wait to serve Elijah. The Holy Spirit says, "Rest up, focus on what I've set before you in the next village, and let's get to business." He tells Elijah to take his eyes off the contradictions and off the lies "because nowhere in my word to you, Elijah, did I say that this heathen queen will destroy you. So stop thinking about her and move on."

The season of contradiction between the offering of God's promise to us and the realization of that promise is incredibly difficult for us to deal with, but I'm telling you now to expect that season of contradiction. I don't know how long that season will last in your life, but you have to be obedient to God and hang on. There is no good or bad work that you can do, no obligation you can perform, in order to speed up or delay God's promises for you. God fulfills His promises in His timing.

The great news is that you have God's word to hang on to, and God's word also says that He is not a liar. You have the freedom to obey, to trust, and to accept God's word and His love even in the midst of your season of contradiction. Simply look the contradiction in the eye and repeat God's promises to you. Remind yourself that He is not a man that He would lie to you. Simply remain obedient in your relationship to Him, and God will fulfill His promises.

Chapter 4: What About Life
BEFORE Death?

When the conversation turns to life after death, my response has always been the same: "Frankly, my dear, I don't give a diddly doo dang."

After death, it's too late.

Here on earth, during the journey of _this_ life, we have the opportunity to enjoy relationship with a living, loving, personal God. The kingdom of heaven doesn't lie on the other side of that curtain we call death; it lies on the other side of accepting your personal relationship with God—no matter how many years of earthly life you have ahead of you when you decide to do so.

The central question of this book, and one we'll return to again and again, is what do the rules and tenets of religion—all those _do dos_ and _don't don'ts_—have to do with gaining access to the kingdom? You might have been told all your life—as so many other Christians and Catholics and Jews and Muslims have been, myself included—that if you stick to the program of _do dos_ and _don't don'ts_, if you scrape by with a passing 60 percent in the test of life, you'll enter into the Kingdom after death. If, on the other hand, you fail, hell is waiting for you. That's the only motivation you're offered for keeping up with this long list of sometimes contradictory, sometimes changing rules.

When people hear that choice, "Follow the rules and the kingdom is open to you, fail to follow them and the gates are shut," they start to confuse its meaning. They start to think, "If I want a relationship with God, I've got to earn it by adhering to these religious dogmas and tenets and rules."

Here is what I want you to understand, if you take nothing else from this book: _the rules have nothing to do with your relationship with God._ Simply by virtue of existing here in this world, you have a relationship with God. You don't need to earn it; you don't need to search for it. It's here, and it's yours.

The moment my children were born, without their having to do a thing, they and I were in relationship. They were born, and voila: instant dad/son relationship. That won't change. No matter what actions they take or what happens to them or me, our relationship is forever sealed by the simple event of their birth.

The same holds true for mankind and our relationship with our God-Father. Our relationship with Him is forever sealed by the act of creation. Its existence is permanent and immutable, but while our *relationship* with God is guaranteed, our *fellowship* with God is not. That's where those rules and tenets come into play.

In any relationship, the individuals involved have to have what I call *functionality*. You might have a relationship with any number of people, from your boss to your next-door neighbor to your spouse, but until you've created a positive, productive functionality with those people, you don't have fellowship with them. Fellowship arises from the decisions you make that foster two-way communication, two-way respect, two-way enjoyment, and two-way productivity within the relationship.

Rules are tools that help us make those positive decisions. Arriving at work promptly at 9 a.m. is a rule that helps you foster fellowship with your boss, curbing your dog is a rule that helps you foster fellowship with your neighbor, and . . . well, I'm sure you can list for yourself all the many, daily rules, large and small, that help you foster fellowship with your spouse.

The same concept is at play in our relationship with the God-Father. We've all got the relationship to start out with, no matter who we are, where we're from, or what we had for breakfast this morning. Now, to go beyond that relationship, we layer on the rules. The rules bring forth order, and order brings forth productive functionality, or *fellowship*.

There it is, plain and simple. God made us for relationship from the beginning and only gave us the rules along the way to enhance our fellowship with Him.

That doesn't mean that to have any sort of fellowship with God, we all have to score 100 percent on the *do do* and *don't don't* exam. I know that I've got fellowship with God. I also know that my fellowship with Him is a process and that it's continuing to grow and to improve, because at this moment, I'm still learning. At this moment, I'm not able to be perfect 100 percent of the time in my behavior with the other knuckleheads called humans. That's just part of how I'm wired, and how we're all wired.

God accepts us and loves us that way, because he made us that way. He gave us our minds, and fortunately for us, those minds have the free will to choose to do certain things and choose not to do other things. That means we'll make mistakes on our journey through life, but in the meantime, if we choose to listen, there are truths out there. There are truths that can help us function positively and productively, that can help us love God with all our hearts, minds, and souls and love others as we want to be loved.

Following that Golden Rule, that rule that trumps all others, is all we need to do to start creating fellowship with God. It's the first and simplest step towards functioning in fellowship and leading a loving, productive, and fulfilling existence here on earth, in this life.

You don't have to wait until your life is over! You don't have to wait until judgment day to see if you've "earned" eternal life or eternal damnation. A lot of people, no matter what religion they come from, have been made to understand that eternal life is something that will happen to them after they die. They do their best to keep up with the *do dos* and *don't don'ts*, and they hope that when they get to the end of the journey, the scales will balance out in their favor. Of course, in the meantime, they're not enjoying the ride—they're too busy keeping score and sweating the small stuff.

What if we could all accept, really know in our hearts, that eternal life is *now*? Well, for starters, we'd all start to have a lot more fun on the ride of life. More importantly, we'd start paying a lot more attention to our fellowship with God here and now, rather than what we hope it might be in the afterlife.

Our fellowship with one another would grow, too. Once you've acknowledged your relationship with God and you've started to build fellowship with Him, you're free to love others, which is just another way of saying that you're free to allow God to act through you. Fellowship with others is God acting through you, and that message spreads. In fact, I'd go so far as to say that the idea of peace on earth could happen if everyone who has a relationship with God (which is to say, everyone) expressed that relationship through fellowship with others.

The catch is, that will never happen in total in our world. God made us with free will, and that means that there will always be some of us who choose *not* to love God and *not* to love each other. This leads to war; it leads to oppression; it leads to sexual predation; it leads to famine; it leads to corruption among the powerful. It's at the heart of all of the world's injustices, and that's, as we discussed in Chapter 2, why our life on this earth is so often called a battle. That's why, here and now, every day, we're exposed to the devil's war.

That does *not* mean that we can't also enjoy the kingdom of heaven here on earth. Sure, God gave us free will, but He didn't do so and then abandon us to our own demise at our own hands. What makes our earthly life an eternal life, what makes our earthly home the kingdom of heaven, is that God has invaded our realm and has invaded our hearts.

He first did this through his law when He miraculously spoke to Moses and delivered the Ten Commandments and the Book of the Covenant. The rules God offered us through that miracle were an olive branch. They were God telling us, "Here's what you need to do in order to function with each other, so that you might have fellowship amongst yourselves. Here, too, is what I want you to do to have fellowship with me."

A lot of those rules had to do with the bloody sacrifice of animals, or what we know as the blood covenant. We all understand some version of the blood covenant from our pop culture. Two little girls, "best friends for life," prick the tips of their fingers and mingle their blood. Now they are "blood sisters." Two Mafiosos cut their wrists and mingle their blood to prove their loyalty and seal their partnership. The act is a symbolic summary of fellowship; it means that two individuals shed their blood as the ultimate covenant with one another, as a way of saying, literally, "What's mine is yours, and what's yours is mine."

When God acted through Moses, He was making that covenant with the Jews. Fellowship is at the root of all of those different kinds of sacrifices and all the rules behind performing them. That, too, is why God tells us in Leviticus 17 that without the shedding of blood, there is no forgiveness of sins. That blood covenant was ultimately consummated in the once-and-for-all sacrifice of Jesus Christ on our behalf.

It used to be that once a year, at the Feast of Atonement, Jews would look to the work of their High Priest for the forgiveness of their sins. The Priest would enter into the Holy of Holies, that most sacred place where the Ten Commandments were kept in the Ark of the Covenant, and, according to the prescribed code of Leviticus, he would sacrifice the animal and spread its blood. He would then come out and lay hands on the scapegoat, symbolizing laying the peoples' sins upon it, and that creature would be driven out into the wilderness to be devoured by wild animals. All the people's sins from the previous year would then be atoned for. That tradition is still alive symbolically in Yom Kippur, but why, today, do we see this sacrifice happen only symbolically? Why hasn't it been in effect for the last two thousand years?

It's not because PETA was formed! The first temple, which housed the Holy of Holies, was destroyed. So, too, was the second temple. Since then, for two thousand years, there has been no sacrifice like the one I described because there has been no proper, by-the-book setting for it.

Without those Temples, you have, quite literally, the "wandering Jew." You have a people who have to follow the rules symbolically, but God is not a symbolic God. His need for relationship didn't change just because the temple changed.

This process of revising the rules is not strictly a Jewish one. The same sort of rule-shifting happens all the time. In fact, I witnessed it happen in Catholicism, and it had a profound effect on my spiritual life. Up until the 1970s, the Catholics abided by the rule of not eating meat on Fridays. The rule was so important that breaking it was considered a mortal sin, as opposed to a venial sin (which earned a slap on the wrist, but was not severe enough to deprive the soul of divine grace) If, on the other hand, you ate meat on Fridays . . . before the 1970s . . . you were bound for eternal damnation.

Well, all of a sudden in the early 1970s, the Catholic Cardinals got together and decided to scrap that rule. Eating meat on Fridays was no longer considered a mortal sin. I was a sophomore in college at the time, and I'm not afraid to confess to you that I was reading *Playboy* magazine.

One day I picked up an issue, and there was a cartoon. It showed a lesser demon coming to Satan and asking something along the lines of, "What the hell are we supposed to do with all these Catholics who ate meat on Friday before they changed the rules?"

Who would have thought I'd find a spiritual epiphany in *Playboy*, but I did.

People see contradictions in the rules like that, as I did, and they think, "Well, we might as well trash-can the Bible."

I'm here to tell you that's the wrong conclusion. What we need to trash-can are our efforts to adhere to those rules *in place of* relationship. We need to trash-can the thinking that tells us, "By following these rules, you can establish a relationship with God."

The Bible isn't going to establish relationship. The rules, whether they come from Leviticus or the New Testament, aren't going to establish relationship. Our relationship with God is pre-established and immutable, whether or not we follow any or all of the rules.

What we need the Bible and its tenets for is to help us function within that relationship. The Bible helps us create order, so that we can enjoy our relationship with God and our relationships with each other. It helps us have fellowship. So, of course, we must not trash-can it, but we *must* trash-can our attempts at taking the Bible and turning it into a scorecard for rule following. We must stop thinking that the four-hundred-some Levitical laws, and the percentage of them we're able to abide by, can earn us our relationship with the God-Father.

It's when we confuse those that we start to wonder, "What degree of perfection is necessary? At what point have I "earned" my relationship with God, and at what point am I the failing student who's going to "flunk," which is to say, lose my spot in the Kingdom of Heaven?"

We start looking at the Bible the way we look at other codes in our lives. For example, say I take a look at my traffic record and see that it's clean and spotless, that I've been following all the rules like a golden boy . . . except for the one time I crossed over the double line from the HOV lane to the regular traffic lanes and got a ticket. Oops, a slap on the wrist—I'm imperfect. Then I have to start wondering, "How many of those little mistakes add up to me losing my license? What kind of *big* mistake would make me lose it in one fell swoop?"

We start to ask ourselves the same kinds of questions about eternal life, and we point to red herrings and say, "But the second temple was destroyed," or "Well, the Cardinals are changing the rules all the time anyway, so why bother? It's all made up, anyway."

That's the equivalent of trying to go it alone—trying to have a relationship with God in the absence of God; somehow trying, futilely and blindly, to have a relationship with God by doing it *our* way, not *His* way. There is absolutely no score we could get on the Biblical scorecard that would earn us a relationship with God if He hadn't already established that relationship for us. We are incapable of creating that relationship, so thank God that God has already done it for us. That means we don't have to be perfect, we just have to accept His provision.

The moment we accept it, we're in the kingdom of heaven, here and now. We have life *before* death. All those rules are secondary. We can follow them to Timbuktu and back again, but we'll still feel empty and ineffectual if we follow them without first acknowledging our pre-existing relationship. So many of us struggle with a sense of emptiness, a sense that we aren't connecting in a real and personal way with our Father, and unfortunately we act on it by struggling even harder for His approval. We work, we donate, and we serve, hoping to gain His blessing.

All that work and money and time doesn't fall under the relationship column. It falls under the fellowship column. It's not a bad thing—don't get me wrong—but it won't earn you Relationship. Relationship is the reward you get before you even hit the track; any reward beyond that is fellowship.

Again, I'll use the parenting example. My kids and I have automatic relationship no matter what. They have my love, guaranteed, but they earn *additional* rewards through their proper behavior. That's what earns them more privileges, a higher allowance, and so forth, because they prove to me through their behavior that they can handle more responsibility and a better fellowship with me. There's no such thing as a better relationship. Relationship is relationship. It's there whether they do their chores and finish their homework or not.

In the same way that I give my kids guidance for improving their behavior and improving fellowship, God has given us guidance. I can turn to any great book, from the teachings of Buddha to the teachings of Mohammed to the great sayings of Solomon in the book of *Proverbs* to the lives and words of the apostle Paul or of Jesus Christ. In each and every one of them, I'll find a tremendous element that's positive and good.

My intention in this book is not to scorn the tenets of religion, or to say that they are useless or harmful when taken by themselves, separately from the misinterpretations and struggles of humans. That is not my message. God created a central good in His process called order. There is no harm in striving to follow that order.

The harm only comes into play when we start believing, and preaching to others, that it is in following that order that we'll be able to start a relationship with God or improve our existing relationship with God, or that, "You'll never have a relationship with God unless you do what's in this Bible the way we tell you that you have to do it."

We don't have to do that at all. Jesus is sitting at the right hand of the Father, and he is ever-living to make intercession between us and our Father. When he walked this earth, he told his band of apostles and students, "You don't want me to leave you, but I'm telling you that it's better for me to leave you and go to our Father in Heaven, so that I can send my spirit back and be with *all* of you who are in relationship with the Father and with me." In his death and resurrection, Jesus sent his spirit out to all the millions of people on earth, for all the generations of history, rather than only reaching the handful of people who sat at the table with his earthly body.

That's how we interface with God. That's how our relationship with Him functions and becomes fellowship. The Holy Spirit is interceding and taking our prayers to God through Jesus Christ, not through Mary or the saints or a priest. To understand God's word, all we have to do is make the decision to trust Jesus to realize it in our lives. If we allow that trust, then we will have continual victory in the series of battles that I call life *before* death. We will have eternal life, and it will begin today.

Chapter 5: Men and Women: Celebrating the Differences

This is a book about relationship. In the previous four chapters, we have delved into the heart of all relationships, the relationship that makes all others possible: our relationship with God. We have talked about what it means to be the recipient of God's unconditional love, and we have talked about how, with God's love as our basis and inspiration, it becomes our duty to love God back with all our might, and to love others as we want to be loved.

It's the second part of that equation that I want to talk about now: *loving others as we want to be loved.* Once we acknowledge that primary, unchanging, ultimate relationship with the God-Father, earthly relationships with other human beings become possible. Once we know what God's unconditional love is, we develop the power and the capacity to give our own unconditional love to others.

The family is the most important place on this earth where you share your unconditional love. You might love your friends, your neighbors, your teammates, your comrades in arms, even your coworkers, but the primary human relationships in your life are those that you have with your family, because family is the earthly mirror we hold up to our relationship with the God-Father. He is our Father in heaven, and we are His children on earth. Our families on earth are the human version of that relationship.

Within our earthly families, we have any number of relationships: parent/child, step-parent/step-child, brother/sister, mother-in-law/son-in-law, grandparent/grandchild . . . the list goes on and on. Of all those relationships, the one between man and wife is central and paramount.

In fact, the husband/wife relationship is so important that I consider this chapter the second most important chapter in this book about relationship.

After the relationship with the God-Father, the husband/wife relationship is the center of order in the universe. Until you've got a stable, productive relationship with your spouse, no other relationship within your family is going to work, and if your family life isn't working, your work relationships and your friendships will suffer for it.

Let's face it, it's easier said than done. If you're anything like any other man or woman on this earth, sometimes you look at your spouse and think, "This person is just so different from me." In that context, how do you set the stage for the best possible communication, the best possible cooperation—the best possible *fellowship*?

You've got the relationship—you exchanged the vows and the rings—and now it's time to move on to building fellowship. Just as we discussed in the previous chapter in terms of your relationship with God, fellowship is what comes second. It's what happens when the relationship starts to create productivity, order, and enjoyment for both people involved, but when you're dealing with creatures as different as men and women, how do you do it? That's what we'll be talking about in this chapter.

Here's what I want you to be aware of before we go any further. Just as religion can stand in the way of our relationship with God, it can also stand in the way of our relationships with our spouses. I've said it before in this book, and I'll say it again: rules, tenets, dogmas, and *religion itself* mean diddly squat in the absence of relationship. Keeping your *do dos* and your *don't don'ts* straight is not going to create a relationship with God. Unconditional love, not religious scorekeeping, is the basis of that relationship. The same holds true in any marriage between man and wife. Following arbitrary rules you get from your marriage counselor or your pastor or your friends isn't going to do a thing for you if you don't have the unconditional love to back it all up.

Let me tell you how I know this to be true. I learned from experience. I've been there, in the "trenches" of marriage, so to speak, and I have seen how the list of *do dos* and *don't don'ts* led me astray. I've also seen how, when my current wife and I threw out everything but our relationship with God and used that unconditional love as the basis and the model, we were awakened to a new level of fellowship. We were awakened to the possibility of being soul mates in God. That's what I want you to have with your spouse.

In Ephesians 5, God gives us the most important principle that all marriages must be built on. "Husbands, love your wives, just as Christ loved the church, and wives, submit to your husbands as to the Lord." Unfortunately, this is one of the most misused and misapplied phrases in the Bible. It has become just another *do do*, and preachers preach it and followers follow it without understanding the heart of it. It gets distorted, and it winds up leading us further away from the fellowship for which we long. So, in this chapter, we'll talk about what this message really means, and what it can do for you in your marriage. I'll start with the half that I understand from my own personal experience as a man, "Husbands, love your wives, just as Christ loved the church." Don't worry, I'll also get to that other tricky phrase, "Wives, submit to your husbands."

What does it mean when God asks men to love their wives as Christ did the church? Well, how did Christ love the church, his body of people? Unconditionally. Gentlemen, God has called upon us to love our wives unconditionally, not because of what we get from them and not because of what we're trying to get from them. We must simply love them.

Loving unconditionally is not instinctual. We have to learn it, first and foremost, by experiencing it ourselves through God's love. Until we acknowledge God's unconditional love, we don't have a prayer of sharing unconditional love here on earth. Second, we have to see this kind of unconditional love modeled through other men. That's usually the part we get hung up on. Guys will tell me, "Great, Randy. I've got my relationship with God. I'm good to go. So why am I still struggling so much in my marriage?" It's because we men are sorely lacking in the mentoring we need from other men. We can't just magically know how to love these diametrically opposed people called our wives, we need to see it done, and more often than not, we see other men doing it poorly or not at all.

I'll give you my own experience as an example. For all of us, it starts out with what we see our dads or our step-dads doing. What I saw growing up in my home was certainly not a man who loved his wife as God loves his children. My father's love for my mother was conditional, and it was even abusive—not physically abusive, but emotionally and verbally. When an issue arose in his marriage, my dad did not know how to handle it from a place of unconditional love. He couldn't, as I call it, "confront his wife in love." Instead, his response was to yell and throw things and use foul language. Where did he learn that? From the mentoring he received from his own father and stepfathers.

Like so many of us, I didn't grow up witnessing a father who loved his wife as Christ loves the church, but I couldn't look to any other role models for an understanding of how to treat women, either. I was the oldest of three boys, I went to an all-boys Catholic school, and I went to college at Loyola University in L.A.—a men's school. All my teachers, all my coaches, all my classmates and all my teammates were men, and of course, I was surrounded by Catholic priests and religious brothers. Then I went immediately into a professional baseball career for eleven years—again, surrounded by men. We didn't have any female shortstops.

In none of those places was I getting the mentoring I needed in how to love women. I didn't have to connect with women on any meaningful level at all. I could enjoy them and then move on to the next port, so to speak. Now, I wasn't a bad guy, but I didn't have to become emotionally involved. I didn't have to learn about giving and receiving affection, and I certainly didn't have to get into the territory of unconditional love.

I didn't want to, anyway. What I was seeing all around me, particularly in my baseball career, was infidelity in marriage. To me, marriage looked like a constant game of deception, and frankly, I didn't want to be bothered. I wasn't sure I would ever want to get married. It wasn't until I was nearly twenty-seven that I finally took the plunge and found myself in completely uncharted waters. I was in over my head.

All my life, growing up surrounded by men, I hadn't been learning affection. I had been learning to fight, to compete, to pick up a sword and cut off heads, to take names, when I was threatened. Now suddenly I was in relationship with a woman, and I found that it wasn't quite what I thought it would be.

I'll never forget hearing a comedian perform about fifteen years ago. He said, "Women, if you would just understand how we're wired, this whole thing would work out much better than it does now. How we're wired is this: we just want lots of sex and to be left alone."

Well, if I had just listened to the men around me, I would have thought that was what marriage would be like, and that if I wasn't getting lots of sex, then there was something wrong with the relationship, and I had better go find the sex elsewhere. Of course, what I was missing, and what a lot of men haven't been properly mentored in, was the affection part of the bargain.

I praise God that I didn't have my own marriage to my wife Crystal tarnished by the "give me lots of sex and leave me alone" syndrome. The truth is that

I didn't want to be left alone! I needed her to connect with me, partner with me and be God's instrument of love to me. And she has fulfilled my longing to be loved – both sexually and emotionally– in a way I never thought possible based on my experience in my single days and during my first marriage. Maturity in Christ does that for you.

Let me attempt to have a little fun with a serious issue that we all face in marriage. I know, guys, we've all got the sex act down mechanically, right? That's instinctual. We're all think we're doing fine in that area, but the moment we get married, there is an introduction to the relational equation called The Expectation of Emotional Availability. The "lots of sex and to be left alone" thing we were expecting? Not happening. Why do they expect us to be intimate? Who the hell taught us that? Certainly not Playboy magazine or swapping stories with our buddies!

In fact, I'd say, in general, we've only got a five-day-a-month window of opportunity in which most women feel emotionally motivated to want sex at all. They may engage us more often than that, but there is an emotional "priming of the pump" that is necessary for that to happen. And, we are woefully emotionally inadequate to "prime that pump" and set the right atmosphere to overcome the kids are acting up, "that time of the month" or she's in a bad mood because they accuse us of things we've done that we are incapable of even thinking of, let alone do!!!

Now, guys, what if I turn the tables on us? What if I asked you what your wife's window of opportunity was each month for getting affection from you? I think we'd all have to admit that it's just as narrow as our window of opportunity for sex, because while the sex is instinctual, the affection isn't. If we haven't seen affectionate relationships modeled by our parents or by other couples we respect, how are we supposed to know how to give and receive affection in our own relationships? I say "give *and* receive" because often it's just as hard for a guy to accept affection from his wife as it is for him to give affection to her. For a lot of men, affection is alien. It delves deep into the heart and the soul, and for someone who's been trained all his life to fight, being that vulnerable doesn't come easily.

That's the position I found myself in when I was first married as a young man. I didn't know how to give and receive affection. In essence, I didn't know how to speak my wife's language. I didn't know it until it was too late, and my first marriage ended in divorce.

Now, if perfection were a prerequisite for teaching or advising, there would be no teachers on this earth. There would be no psychologists or theologians or pastors or rabbis or professors or doctors or lawyers. If you had to be perfect before you ever offered someone advice, you wouldn't dare open your mouth or put pen to paper. None of us is batting a thousand in this life. We *all* fall short of God's perfection. So, as I write this chapter, I realize that I am touching on areas in which I have been woefully inadequate in my own life. Like the overweight doctor telling his patients to get into shape, I'm not always able to practice unconditional love in my own marriage. I never got there with my first wife, and it is a daily struggle with my second wife. I'm asking you to learn to celebrate the differences between men and women, but I will freely admit that I, too, am still learning. It is a struggle.

That struggle comes from our believing that there's a starting point to love. "If you would just do this for me, then I'll give you the love you're asking for." What you end up with is a man and a woman chasing each other in a circle, hollering after each other.

"You do this first!"

"No, you do this first!"

Is that how God does things? No. He jumped in the ring from the get-go and said, "I'm here for you. Forget the *do dos* and the *don't don'ts*, I'm just gonna love you. You can love me back or not; I'm not going to make you. I'm not asking for anything in return for my love."

Men, in our relationships with our wives, it's time for us to stop running around in that endless loop. It's time for us to enter that circle first, without expecting our wives to be there before us or even hoping that they'll join us after the fact. It's our job to step in and say, "I love you, and I'm not asking for anything back." Before we know it, we *will* get love and fellowship in return—more than we ever bargained for in the first place.

That's what God means when he asks us to love our wives as Christ loved the church.

❧

Now, I promised I'd get to the hard part—the "wives, submit to your husbands" part. Men have used that command for years to defend everything from arranged marriages to domestic violence. I've heard guys say, "My wife should have sex with me whenever I want because she's supposed to submit to me." I've heard them say, "She's going to go live wherever I find a job or get transferred because she's supposed to submit to me." Or how about, "She's Catholic and I'm Lutheran, but our kids are going to be raised Lutheran no matter what, because I'm the man"?

Okay. That's one way of interpreting it, but what happens when we add the other half of the equation back in? "Wives, submit to your husbands, *and* husbands, love your wives as Christ loved the church." God's way of loving us is to give us free will. We're welcome to choose for ourselves, and if we choose to stray, He's there waiting for us to return. If we choose to follow Him, our fellowship grows and increases.

So, if I'm not upholding my end of the deal and loving my wife unconditionally, I've got no business quoting scripture to her and telling her to submit. If, on the other hand, I *am* upholding my end of the deal and always confronting my wife in love, odds are she's going to want to meet me in the circle.

That's why *submission* and *respect*, in this context, are interchangeable concepts. Think of it this way, in terms of what God says to all people, and then we'll take it back to the specifics. God wants all people, men and women, to understand that they have relationship with Him, to accept that, and then to move on to greater fellowship with Him. They achieve that fellowship through order. Without that order, you have people following rules willy-nilly, guessing at what they think is right, and you never get to productive functionality.

The same holds true in the relationship between man and wife. The unconditional love—meeting in the circle—has to happen first, and until that happens, no amount of ordering each other around is going to make the relationship function productively. Once you have unconditional love, however, everything else will fall into place behind it. You will *want* to work together, as a team, of your own free will.

That's what God means when he asks women to respect their husbands. You can't have fellowship without order. So, God isn't saying that women need to do whatever their husband says, whether the husbands are acting out of love or not. To do that would in fact be promoting chaos, not order, but God did create men and women with distinct roles and distinct emotional and physical lives, and when we respect and celebrate those differences, we create order and fellowship.

Remember the comedian who said, "Men want lots of sex and to be left alone"? I think he actually had it wrong. Men don't want to be left alone; they want a cheerleader. God equipped us to be the fighters, the disciplinarians, to go out into the world and defend our wives and families, and to create order in the realms that are our homes. What we want from our wives is to feel that we are respected and loved and appreciated for fulfilling that role.

Basically, we want a lot of "attaboys" from our wives.

It's what we've wanted since we were boys, showing off on our bikes for the girls. I distinctly remember trying to kick the ball over the fence in kindergarten just to impress this one little girl. I continued to try to impress girls through sports my whole life. Other guys do it with music, or with their mental acuity, or with the amount of money they have. Men are always trying to impress women, and when we don't get the "attaboys" in return, that's when the relationship goes off-kilter for us.

If, however, a man knows that his wife is going to respect him and cheer for him, that's when he'll be even more motivated to put all of himself into the relationship and into fighting for his family. Whatever the man is doing to earn money to care for his family, he needs to know that his wife respects the physical effort or the mental effort he's putting in. Then everything he does in terms of working for the family and making decisions for the family will be based, on the one hand, on his unconditional love, and on the other hand, on the knowledge he has that his wife will respect and admire him.

This doesn't mean that men are the lords of women, but in the realm of the household, the man is king—and the woman is queen. It is the man's duty not only to uphold his God-given role as king of his realm, but also to uphold his wife's God-given role as queen. Even as he's acting as king and creating order for his family, he'd also better make sure that everyone in that family (and everyone outside it) knows that she is his queen. His friends have got to know it, his boss has got to know it, and above all else, his children have got to know it. He's got to tell them, "This woman is the queen of my realm, and you'll treat her as such, " and if anyone doesn't, there will be hell to pay. That's how a husband is responsible for letting his wife know that she is loved and cherished—not just through the affection he shows her, but also by being prepared to launch a thousand ships to defend her.

On the journey of marriage, we will certainly get sidetracked. I don't care how much you love God, or how much feel loved by God, or how much you want to love your spouse as you love yourself. We are all imperfect, and we will all struggle, but that's why this chapter is called *Celebrating the Differences*. It is only after conflict that we can begin to see those differences for what they are, rather than trying to hide them or ignore them. That's when we'll be best equipped to return to true north, God's word. That's when we'll truly celebrate what a mighty God we serve—a God capable of creating such difference, and yet such balance. Through God, we'll have the capacity to celebrate our spouses as we ourselves want to be celebrated and to love them as we want to be loved.

Chapter 6: Raising
Sane Kids in an Insane World

Imagine a large umbrella, too large for any single person to hold. It's wide enough to shelter your whole family from a heavy rain, and it's strong enough to hold up against even the strongest of winds. Let's call that umbrella "God's protection."

Underneath it are you, your spouse, and all of your children. As long as each of you stays under that umbrella, you are sheltered by God's way, but the moment you step out from under it, you create chaos. The chaos doesn't just affect you; it ripples outward and touches the lives of every other person under that umbrella with you.

Now, simply by virtue of the fact that the umbrella exists and you exist, you are in relationship with God. You don't have to do anything to earn that relationship. You don't have to hold the umbrella the right way; you don't have to polish its handle twice in the morning and twice at night; you don't even have to stay underneath it. The relationship is there, no matter what you do, and whether you like it or not.

Fellowship comes with staying under the umbrella. It comes with maintaining order and following God's way. Luckily for us, God has given us very clear instructions for the order He wants us to maintain under His umbrella. As we discussed in the previous chapter, God tells us in Ephesians 5, "Husbands, love your wives, just as Christ loved the church, and wives, submit to your husbands as to the Lord." He has given us a second imperative, too. He tells us in the fifth commandment, "Honor thy father and mother."

From these two simple instructions, we know that there is a chain of command under the umbrella: first God, then the husband, then the wife, then the kids. If the husband strays out from under the umbrella, he disturbs its balance, and he lets the wind and rain fall on his family. The same holds true for the wife and for the children. Whenever anyone strays, the whole umbrella tips, and the whole family is affected.

In other words, the moment you violate your fellowship with God, it becomes impossible for you to have fellowship with other human beings.

That's what I'm talking about when I call this chapter "Raising Sane Kids in an Insane World." Let's face it, there are a lot of temptations in the world that, if we succumb to them, might cause our umbrellas to tip.

In this chapter, we'll first take a look at the problem, the "insane world," and then we'll take a look at the solution: how can we raise our children with both unconditional love and a firm, godly hand?

Before we can even start talking about raising kids, we've all got to acknowledge that we're all basically kids ourselves. First and foremost, we're God's kids. So, we've got no business going around making decrees for our children here on earth, if we aren't first making sure we're in good with our Father in heaven.

For many of us, that's no simple task. It is our job as parents to model unconditional love and open, honest, firm fellowship for our children, but how can we model these things if we never saw them modeled ourselves? If we were never parented in the image of the God-Father, how can we parent with godliness ourselves?

A lot of this stems from a single rough period in our nation's history. My father was a product of the 1920s, raised by parents who experienced the trauma of World War I. He grew up during the Depression, and was a young man through World War II and the Korean War. He and hundreds of thousands of men like him were deeply impacted. Their ability to emotionally connect with their children, with their wives, and most importantly with God was stunted.

These men, improperly fathered by their own dads and then traumatized by war and economic depression, became fathers to a whole generation of boys who inherited their problems. It became a vicious cycle of emotional and spiritual immaturity. What's most tragic about the situation is that the way out of the cycle is through God, but these men have learned to be mistrustful of any kind of fatherhood. When men who couldn't trust their earthly fathers hear their pastors and their wives and their friends saying, "Put your faith in your Heavenly Father," it's only natural that they think, "That's not for me."

But whether we like it or not, we are all God's kids. I'm no exception! Here I am, nothing more than a big kid with hair on my chest, and suddenly it's my job to parent children. I'm facing the same issues I did forty years ago when I was running around the house in Superman pajamas. I'm confronting uncharted territory, unfamiliar relationships, and a need for security. I've also got three sons and a stepson who are all facing the same issues and looking to me for the answers.

Just like them, I need parenting and guidance. If I'm willing and able to turn to God and listen to his word and his Spirit showing me the way, then my family and I will do all right. We'll all stay under that umbrella, and I will be able to shelter my wife and children as God shelters me. But what if, due to generations of inherited strife, I just don't know how to step up and be the man?

That's exactly the position most men have found themselves in over the last fifty years. As a result, it has fallen to women to be both mothers and fathers, but as we discussed in Chapter 5, God gave men and women separate roles, and we should honor and celebrate them. There are things that women can provide for their children that men cannot, and there are things that men can provide for their children that women cannot.

So we've got a generation of kids being raised by mothers who are doing double duty because their husbands are out to lunch emotionally. No matter how well meaning or devoted those women might be, they just can't be everything for their children. The result is a whole host of kids who aren't getting the kind of masculine, physically assertive discipline that they need and can only get from a father figure.

Now we add to the mix the financial pressures, the job pressures, the inherent differences between men and women—all the things we talked about in Chapter 5 that can create tension between man and wife. What we get is the breakdown of the American family.

We all know the statistics. We've all read that 50 percent of first marriages end in divorce and that the percentage rate only climbs higher for second and third marriages. We drag our kids along behind us into these dysfunctional situations. Worse yet, we stay in the marriages because we want to be good Christians and we want to provide a stable home for our children. Little do we know that we're only modeling more dysfunction for them. How can you teach your children to love unconditionally when they're witnessing your spouse emotionally abuse you? How can you teach your children to be faithful when they're witnessing your spouse run around behind your back? How can you teach your children to love and nurture themselves when they're witnessing your spouse's addiction?

That's the insanity I'm talking about. That's our world today: parents who are unable to model godliness for their children, spouses who are at odds, divorce, abuse, absenteeism.

You don't really need me to list these problems, do you? You're already well aware of them. If you thought everything was honky-dory and easy as pie in the area of raising children, you would have skipped this chapter.

So let's move on. Let's get beyond naming the problems and get to solving them. Don Henley had a great song, "Get Over It." That's exactly what this chapter is about. If you're going to play the victim, you're never going to be the victor. So how do you leave the past in the past and become the victor in the parenting arena?

One of the central themes of this book has been the importance of understanding the difference between *relationship* and *fellowship*. That concept is crucial in this chapter. You've got relationship with your children by virtue of the fact that they were born. It's a done deal; the relationship is there, and you don't have to do anything more or anything less to maintain it. You *are* responsible for building *fellowship*, or order and positive functionality within the relationship. That's where things get tricky because proper parenting is not instinctual. Sure, the act of conceiving a child is, but we all know there's a lot more to it than that. Actually raising a child is not inherent to the human condition. It's a learned skill.

All you know is that you love this kid unconditionally, but you have to *learn* to show that love. You have to learn it by observing how your parents loved you, disciplined you, communicated with you, mentored you, and encouraged you. You have to watch others passing on their strength and their spiritual values to you before you can turn around and pass on those things to your children.

Lucky for us, we don't just have our earthly parents as models. We've also got our Heavenly Father. No matter what we do, no matter how we mess up, we've got relationship with Him and we've got His unconditional love. That's the good news. The moment you accept God's unconditional love as an unchanging and non-negotiable part of your life, you'll be capable of providing unconditional love as an unchanging and non-negotiable part of your children's lives. Once you experience it for yourself, you'll be capable of creating the experience for them.

Your fellowship with God comes from creating order in your life by following His way, and you know His way both by opening yourself to His Spirit within you, and by following his word. He's the manufacturer of the vehicle you're riding in, so it only makes sense to read the owner's manual He provided for you. You'll find out pretty quickly that the rules are simple: the gas pedal makes it go; the brake pedal makes it stop. The moment you violate the system He provided, you can't have order.

It works the same way with your kids. The relationship is there no matter what, and it's up to you to forge fellowship by creating order in your home. The first step is for you to cut yourself some slack and understand where your source of strength comes from. It doesn't come from some magic place inside you. It doesn't come from your spouse. It doesn't come from your children. It doesn't come from the position you hold at work or how much money you make. The source of your strength is God.

And thank God it's God! That makes everything a whole lot easier for you, if you're willing to shut up and listen. You don't have to guess at the right path to follow. You don't have to be Dr. Spock or Dr. Phil. All you have to do when you need to recharge your battery is go back to God's will. When you don't know how to parent your children because you were imperfectly parented yourself, you've got the word of God, the Bible, to show you the way. I promise you, God will never intend for us to do anything without giving us the specific ability, through his word, to get the job done.

The most important clue we've got is still the Golden Rule. *Love God, and love others as you want to be loved.* In this case, that translates to, "How would you want to be raised, if you were those kids?"

Think of it this way. At the end of your life, when you're on your deathbed, what are you going to want to remember about your life? Are you going to want to call your family and friends to your side so that you can tell them about your smart investments? Are you going to want to review your estate plan or your stock portfolio with them? Are you going to make a list for them of all the houses and toys you earned for yourself?

Or will you simply want to say, "I enjoyed and made the most of the relationships God gave me"?

I'm pretty sure you'll be more focused on the latter, and I guarantee you, it's what your kids will care about, too. At your funeral, they will want to be able to say, "He was a great dad. He provided, he sacrificed, he loved. Sure, he could have driven a nicer car, he could have owned vacation properties, but he decided that spending time with us and knowing what was going on in our lives was more important than his clients or his company or his retirement account."

I don't know about you, but I don't know of any kids who are going to sit there at their dad's funeral and say, "Well, it's okay with me that he wasn't around. Look at how big our inheritance is!"

To get started on building that fellowship—the kind that will make your kids say, "He was a great dad," or "She was a great mom," at your funeral—all you have to do is go back to the Golden Rule. Even if you didn't experience unconditional love growing up, the concept of loving and treating others like you want to be treated gives a solid foundation to build upon.

The second most important thing to be sure of is that your spouse is coming from the same foundation—that he or she is as firmly rooted in God's way as you are.

Here's the bottom line: if you're paired with a spouse who refuses to join you under God's umbrella, get out. Get back to God. You don't have to live in His absence just because your spouse is choosing to do so. More importantly, neither do your children. Everything that happens under that umbrella trickles down to them, so don't allow ungodliness to be their model.

Once both you *and* your spouse are solid in your relationships with God, you'll be capable of modeling unconditional love to your children. What's next? Discipline. Yes, your primary role when raising children is to provide unflinching love, but that doesn't mean coddling or babying or being permissive. Part of loving your children in the image of the God-Father is knowing how, with a firm but gentle hand, to return them to a righteous path when they have strayed.

God gives us a basic outline of how to do this in Ephesians 6:4. "And, ye fathers, provoke not your children to wrath: but bring them up in the nurture and admonition of the Lord.' God asks us to discipline our children, but to do it with love, because that's how He disciplines us.

God disciplines me all the time, and let me tell you, it's not easy. When the Holy Spirit convinces me that I'm out of order, that I've strayed out from under God's umbrella, it's painful. It pricks my heart, but I can always feel God's love acting in my life, and I can always trust that God won't punish me arbitrarily.

I can draw a direct line of cause and effect between my behaviors and the consequences I reap from God. When I'm out of order, I can expect to find a manifestation of that chaos in the physical world. If I'm drinking too much or using drugs, should I be surprised to find that I run into health problems? If I'm abusing my body by overeating, should I be surprised when I'm overweight and facing high cholesterol or diabetes or heart problems? If I'm running around with my secretary, should I be surprised when my wife leaves me and takes my children with her?

If I'm failing to be a man of God, there are consequences, and just as that law of cause and effect holds true in my relationship with God my Father, it holds true in my children's relationship with me, their earthly father. When kids are out of line, there must be consequences.

The flipside is true in both relationships as well. When I'm in proper fellowship with God, I can expect to reap the rewards. That doesn't necessarily mean that suddenly wealth will fall at my feet and all of my relationships will become easy and rewarding, but it does mean that I can release fear and know that I am resting under the umbrella of God's protection.

My children know the same thing about *my* protection. No matter what happens, they know that I am their protector. They know that if someone out there disrespects them, threatens them, abuses them, or misuses them . . . God help that individual. I am the king of the domain that God gave me, and my kids know it and are secure in my protection. I model that absolute protection for them in the same way that God models it for me.

At the same time, protecting my children doesn't mean that I'm going to be permissive with them any more than my having God's protection means that I can get away with anything I want. I protect my children, but I still discipline them. However, I always keep in mind God's imperative: "Fathers, provoke not your children to wrath."

I spanked each of my three boys when they were little—once. With each one, I only had to do it once, and the matter was settled. They never tested me again. I'll give you an example. About two years after my divorce from my first wife, I took my three boys on a shopping trip with me to Circuit City. They were seven, five, and three years old at the time.

My middle son was acting up and playing with things on shelves that I had asked him not to touch. So I took his hand away from the shelf, and his response was to scream. Loudly.

I turned to the salesperson and pointed at my seven-year-old son and my toddler in his stroller, and I asked, "Would you watch these two for a moment?"

He agreed, and so I took my five-year-old to the bathroom. I had no intention of embarrassing him in front of the salesperson and everyone else in the store. I wanted him to understand that this was between he and I.

When we got to the bathroom, I lifted him up and put him on the counter. Can you imagine if suddenly your boss who's unhappy with your performance or a police officer pulling you over for speeding were fifteen feet tall? That's what it's like for a child to look up at their mother or father, and let me tell you, that's scary. So I put him up on the counter so he could look me in the eye.

I said, "This is the rule. You will not scream at me so you can get your way. That's not how things are going to be done between us. Ever. Do you understand?"

He did understand.

Then I lovingly lifted him off the counter and put him over my lap, so that I wouldn't hurt his back. I pulled his pants down and gave him one firm swat on his bare bottom. Then I pulled his pants back up and kissed him.

I said, "I love you, and that's why I did this."

And I never had to do it again.

Each of my three boys had a defining moment like that. They decided to test me, and I let them know—gently, lovingly, but *firmly*—what the parameters were.

You know and I know that we live in modern times. Many of us, if not *most* of us, now live in households with not just our own biological children, but also our spouse's children from a previous marriage. So how do you handle matters of discipline when you're dealing with a stepchild?

God tells us that the man is the head of the household. He is king of the realm, and his wife is queen, and that designation stands, whether he is the biological father of every child in the realm or not. When my stepson is under my roof, he knows to respect me as king, but he also knows that when he's in his father's home, his father is king. My boys know the same thing of their stepfather.

Too often, a divorce starts a power war. Kids get used as bait, as ammunition, and as shields. Each spouse tries to "win" over the other, and they use their own children to score points, but you know what? In a divorce, there is no "winning." There's only loss: loss of your dreams, loss of your financial stability, loss of control.

The only way to regain any semblance of control is to keep returning to true north–God's word. Keep returning to that Golden Rule. When my ex-wife was remarrying, I went to her new husband and said, "There will be times when my boys will come live in your kingdom. They're my kids, and they know that I'm their dad and their spiritual head, but they also know that when they're in your realm, you are the king. I will back you up as the king, as long as what's happening in your house isn't detrimental to my children and their spiritual development. I have too much respect for the role God has called you to play in your household to violate it. If my boys disobey your rules, you let me know, and I'll deal with it."

In twenty years, we've never had any kind of conflict.

The same holds true with my relationship to my stepson's father. The exception is that I honor his position as his son's ultimate spiritual guide, and so I have never disciplined his son physically.

There did come a time, however, when my stepson tested me just as my biological sons did. He was thirteen years old, a seventh grader, and he was starting to think of himself as a man. One evening, I heard him in the other room tell my wife—his mother—to f****** off.

I walked straight into that room, and calmly, lovingly, I said, "Pack your bag and get in the car. We're going to talk to your dad."

His eyes got as big as saucers, and my wife didn't know what I was going to do, but she respected my position as king of the realm and honored my judgment. We both understand that God has called me, as the man, to handle matters of discipline.

My stepson and I got into the car. I didn't slap him or intimidate him or cuss at him. I just took him over to his dad's house. When his father answered the door, I told him, "Your little boy here who thinks he's a man just told my wife to f****** off. Is that acceptable to you?"

"Absolutely not," he said.

"Then I'm giving him over to you to discipline as you see fit," I said.

That was it. Again, just like with my own sons, we've never had an issue since.

This is why it's so critical for children to have a father figure in their lives. God has given me the ability to discipline. Remember when the baseball team manager in *Bull Durham* is frustrated that the players won't listen? The veteran player Crash Davis tells him, "They're kids. Scare 'em." The next scene is hilarious, with the manager storming into the locker room, kicking bats across the floor, and hollering at the naked players huddled in the shower.

The scene has a real point, too. Discipline is ineffectual without the real possibility of punishment to back it up. That's why God gives the role of disciplinarian to men. He tells us in Proverbs 13:24, "Whoever spares the rod hates his son, but he who loves him is diligent to discipline him." Men are capable of fulfilling that imperative.

Women want to debate; provide for "time outs"; it's their nature. Men, on the other hand, are willing to step in and say, "I'm not here to debate this."

Women want to use psychological warfare, but on undeveloped four-, five-, and six-year-old brains, it simply doesn't work. Loving, *physical* discipline works.

Now I'm not saying that because God says, "Don't spare the rod," we need to go out and beat our kids to a pulp, but we do need to provide the threat of punishment to back up the discipline. Women aren't equipped to do this. Men are.

It's unfortunate that so many women in this country have been left to raise children on their own, either because they're single or because their husbands have checked out emotionally. The result is that for the last thirty years, our children have been raised under the influence of female psychology. The only discipline they've gotten is, "Oh, you better not do that" or, "I'm going to count to three." Educators, coaches, and employers will all tell you that we're now dealing with a self-absorbed and emotionally and spiritually weak generation as a result.

But we men can't fill both roles either! Men, particularly those raised by fathers who were products of the Depression and World War II, as I discussed, have got a lot of emotional catching up to do. They need their wives as models for emotional depth. No woman wants to submit to a selfish and emotionally stunted dumb-ass, but women *do* want to submit to a man of God. They're wired that way.

When both partners can recognize and fulfill their God-given roles, everything falls into place. Life under the umbrella is balanced. But ultimately, whether we live in traditional families or blended families, parenting is a team sport. Men can't do it without women, and women can't do it without men.

None of us can do it without God. It's a tough job, but we've got a true north to come back to, time and time again: God's word. If we stick with it, we can't fail. It's there to protect us, to encourage us, to enhance us, and to make us productive and functional in our relationship with Him and with each other. Violate His word, and you've got an insane world, but stick with Him, and see if He doesn't guide you, instruct you, fulfill you, and pour His blessings upon you. Stick with God's Word, and you'll find the path to raising sane kids.

Chapter 7: Work and Home: Finding a Balance

Think of your life's foundation as a three-legged stool. The stool's three legs support our lives: that's our finances, our relationships, and our overall health.

In my last book, *Safe Money System*, I focused on finances and the proper way to address them. You've got to control your finances; they can't control you, but what normally happens when we finally get a hold of our finances is that we forget the other two aspects of the three-legged stool.

If our relationships are off-kilter, everything is off-kilter.

This chapter addresses the issues related to the balance between work and home in your marriage. As we talk about this balance, I'll use the assumption that you're faithful, honest, authentic, and unconditional lovers of your spouse and family. Of course, you're not perfect. Nobody is, but this is the basic premise I'll use because if you've got all the other issues of infidelity and selfishness—if you're not taking the time to be with your kids on the weekend because you think you have to play golf, or if you'd rather play poker three nights a week than be there for your kids—then that's another issue. You're already out to lunch and you're going to be paying for the lunch of your spouse's attorney some day as well.

Most of my clients and the good, faithful men I know live under an assumption or a preconceived notion that has been passed down for generations from our grandfathers and our fathers: "If I'm providing for the family, I'm doing my job, and hopefully that's enough."

When a man has been raised with this assumption, he believes that if he's making a good living and has to work 60 hours a week or travel to do what he has to do, then that's more than enough. Most men will inevitably face conflicts that arise out of that way of thinking. These conflicts can come from an increase in hours spent at work, constant relocations demanded by corporations, or even a layoff. A new issue, also, is the idea that a 30-year-old today will probably have at least 5 different jobs for 5 different kinds of companies before he reaches age 65.

These conflicts cause nothing but insecurity in the household, and when that insecurity affects a man's wife and his children, he is not being what God called him to be, which is the head of the domain and the head of the house. He'll have to abdicate much of that responsibility of being the head of the domain to his wife because he doesn't have the time to fulfill that role when money calls. What results is a lack of effective discipline for the kids. The effort of discipline might be there, but the effectiveness of discipline, which comes from the difference between men being men and women being women as addressed in chapter 6, is missing.

I've been on business trips where I've had to call home and deal with the kids over the phone. I was away, but the important thing was that it was their father dealing with them. You don't have to be physically present to dish out the discipline and the stability that your kids—and frankly, your wife—need. So if your wife knows that you might be traveling or you might be working late, but if she needs you (within reason), you will take her phone call and, because you're authentic, you will let your business partners, clients, coworkers, and employees know that your family is more important than your job, and that your walk with God is more important than your family, which is more important than your job.

Now, this doesn't mean you read the Bible for seven hours a day and give your job one. That's not what God is calling for. Being the head of your family and maintaining a proper balance between work and home is about *attitude* more than it is about *activity*.

Back when phone calls were cheaper, a wealthy guy, my first guide in the financial world, told me that lack of wealth is when you need a dime to make a phone call to save your life and you don't have one on you. Wealth is an extremely subjective concept. Wealth, by definition, has to do with having more money. A wealthy person is presumably someone who has stopped working and has more money coming in than money going out, more income than outcome. This can be ten billion in, eight out. It can be five grand in, three out, but as long as you've got more in than out, and you're not working anymore, you're wealthy. It's not the amount that matters. It's attitude.

Focusing on the amount, or the activity, puts you in the mindset that says, "I just don't have the time; I'm sorry, I commute an hour and a half; I have to put in my 8 to 10 hours; I have to work Saturday." These are the situations that arise as we adjust our lives to try to get to where we want to be in life to be effective lovers of our spouses and kids, take part in their sports activities, music, and open houses, and provide the things and the time that kids need and always remember about their parents. This is where we have to prime the pump on that life we're working toward—that future life, that desired life. We do that with the proper attitude.

Taking the right steps toward the life we want by maintaining the proper attitude and the right foundation goes right back to what we've discussed throughout this book.

That proper foundation—that proper relationship with God, and therefore, a proper fellowship and functional relationship with our kids, our friends, our spouse, and so forth—is Biblically based. Nowhere in the Bible does it say that you are to forsake your responsibility as a husband and a father to improve your bottom line on your financial statement.

In chapter 3, we discussed relationships and obligations. Obligations influence the way we operate in relationships. If you are led to believe that you are obligated to make x amount of dollars in order for your wife to respect you, love you, and not want to leave you for someone making more money, you're screwed right out of the gate. Why? Because you'll never make enough money.

John Bogle, who started the financial firm The Vanguard Group, wrote a book called *Enough*. In this book, he tells the story of a party on Long Island in the Hamptons at the massive home of a rich hedge fund guy. At the party are Joseph Heller, who wrote the novel *Catch-22*, and someone else. The other guy says to Heller, "You know, this guy makes more in a week than you have made in your entire lifetime from *Catch-22*."

Heller says, "Yeah, except I have something he'll never have." The other guy says, "What's that?" Heller says, "Enough."

Solomon said in a proverb that men will always spend in excess of the money they make., but God wants us to beat that pattern. He doesn't want us to spend more than we make, but people do.

The only way that I've ever managed not to spend more than I make is to give. Give God his dime on the dollar. Give myself a dime on the dollar in the bank, then go ahead and spend the rest of it on what needs to be spent.

I've found that people who are givers never abuse a budget. A giver won't go out and buy a Ferrari he can't afford. Givers always think, "I'm giving God his money. I'm putting money away for my family and my future. What does my wife and my family need?" Givers put themselves last. A giving heart is always last in the equation.

When you're others-centered, the paradox is that you'll always be taken care of with more love, affection, and respect from God as he blesses the people and situations in your life, from friends to family to work. When you have the proper perspective and proper mechanics of living life His way by sowing and reaping and being a good steward of your finances, which we will get into later in this chapter, you will always have enough money.

You'll never know how much is enough because how much is enough depends on your attitude. It's never the amount of work, but the attitude that goes into the work that matters.

The basic concept of the scriptures and the teachings of Jesus was this: the integrity of a man of God can be seen through his ability to work and do unbelievable work as though he were doing that work unto God himself. This doesn't make a difference whether you're a shoeshine kid or the CEO of a corporation. The attitude is the same. When you adopt this attitude, your work takes on new meaning. I've always told my kids to remember two things no matter what job they're doing, whether they're 15, 25, or 55 years old. First, remember that you're always in audition for the next promotion that God will give you. You never know for whom you're doing the service, whether you're bagging groceries, working in a bank, doing financial retirement planning, writing a book, or being a CEO of a company. You can never predict whether that person for whom you're doing the service will look at you and think, "That is a quality person; I want him on my team."

The second important thing I always tell my kids is that whatever the duty might be, do it as though you own the company. If you have to arrange the mailroom, arrange the mailroom. If you have to do deliveries, do the deliveries. If the boss gives you letters to type out, type them as if you run the company, because some day you may if you do things right.

God will promote you as you do your work with responsibility and balance. This is not only what God looks for, but also what others look for, and these others might be people God brings across your path to promote you.

What does this have to do with work and the home and the balance necessary to keep a good life? This balance goes hand-in-hand with always trying to do things for other people, for your employer or your employees, for your clients, your customers, or your partners. You can only do this if you model this life, speak it, and live it everywhere, especially in your home. Your wife and kids, and all the people you will take with you when you die, are more important than the futile dollar bill that you won't be able to take.

If this is a truth, why don't we balance our lives with this truth in mind? If the truth is that all the supposed treasures of this life interfere with a productive fellowship with our wife and kids, and with our friends and our families, then why don't we adopt new attitudes toward our work?

If we operate out of the right perspective, our families will look at us and say, "Dad is working extra hours this week, but we feel secure that he loves us," or, "If dad doesn't show up to a game that he normally shows up to, then there's a darn good reason, because dad is consistent." Why? Because you've been honest with your kids along the way. You've told them, "This is where I'm at. This is how much you mean to me," and told your spouse, "This is where I'm at. This is how much you mean to me." This is how you exhibit a balance of love. Maybe you have to work late one night, but maybe you go home with flowers or tell your spouse that when you get home, you're going out to dinner. Whatever the case may be, the important thing is to let your family know that even though the activity precludes the quality time you get to spend with them, they know that your attitude always speaks, "You guys are the most important priority in my life. Not this job."

In this generation, women are very active in the marketplace, too, but hopefully both spouses aren't working to the detriment of the kids. This is an issue that must be banged out under the philosophy of loving others as you want to be loved. When you were growing up, did you want the nanny raising you or did you want your mom and dad there? This is all part of that balance between work and home.

Let me tell you a story about my wife Crystal and how she balanced her work with her life. A couple years before she met me, my wife got divorced, had a two-year-old baby, and had to take that baby to daycare because she worked at a computer distribution company and made six figures a year. Crystal had to take care of herself and the baby because she wasn't getting a whole lot of support from her ex.

What happened? Her son had to go to daycare at 6 o'clock and then was picked up at 6 o'clock because that's what Crystal had to do to survive. She also hired a nanny every now and then to take care of the kid until he was almost four years old and could go to preschool. Then he was in preschool for twelve hours a day.

When I met Crystal, she continued to work for about a year and a half until the tech meltdown happened in the late '90s, early 2000s. Then Crystal and I sat down to talk about her situation, and she expressed to me the frustration and guilt she felt regarding her kid. She didn't want to continue feeling these negative feelings, which came from not being available to be with her kid. Crystal couldn't take her son to school. She couldn't be there when he got home. She could tell that at five or six years old, her son was an athlete. Would she be there for his games? Would she be able to take him to practices and pick him up? Or was she going to tell him some day, when he's older, "I'm sorry I had to work until 6 so I could make an extra ten grand a year."

It was difficult for Crystal to decide to trust God. She asked me, "How am I going to get a part-time job?" At that point, we knew I could take care of the family because God blessed me and answered my prayers with the ability to do so without her having to work. Crystal's question was, "How am I going to find a part-time job that allows me to take the kid to school in the morning, pick him up when he gets home, be there at night, not have to travel," and the list continued.

Within a month, Crystal and I went to a couples' retreat through our church. We were sitting and having beers with one of our buddies who owned a company. He began talking about his company and said, "Man, I could really use somebody like Crystal with her talent at my company." Crystal said, "You're kidding." He said no, he wasn't. A week or two later, Crystal started working from 10 o'clock to 3:30 or 4 PM—part-time, no pressure, and she enjoyed it. The job got Crystal out of the house, which she needed because she's a hard charger who always did well in her life, took care of herself, and wanted her own money. Eventually, that deal ended, and then another ended, and now she's a personal assistant for a very successful Mary Kay distributor.

Now Crystal only has to work 3 days a week for 3 hours each day. She makes enough money, is satisfied, helps somebody, and she has never missed one game for her kid. She has never missed one practice, one open house, or one discussion with the principal or the teacher, in the last 10 years. She trusted God. She has balance. Her kid will never look back and say, "Wasn't this great, my nanny raised me, and I can't wait for my nanny to be there to give me away at my wedding."

Balance is a trust game. Trust in God. This trust entails faith, and faith happens when the things you hope for become realized, when the things you hope for become reality.

When I was growing up, my dad worked in southern California as a lineman. I remember vividly that my mom didn't have to work, and made it to every one of my games and my two brothers' games. To this day, I appreciate that she was there. I dedicated my first book to my mom and dad, and I said to them, "Thanks for being there. Thanks for taking part in my life and thanks for caring enough to do so."

In high school, I was the big man on campus and fortunate enough to do really well, then go on to play professional baseball. I remember I'd be pitching a game in high school and sometimes my dad would be there, but a lot of times he couldn't because he worked. An Edison lineman worked from 8 to 5 with one hour off. The games were at three. The area in Gardena where we lived fell within the borders of where he worked on utility poles as a lineman. I remember several games in which I'd be pitching a game in the 1st or 2nd inning and Dad wasn't at the game yet. Nothing was more inspiring than looking up from the mound to see that big yellow Edison truck roaring into the parking lot. I still choke up just thinking about it, and his dedication to sharing my life.

Of course, there'd be an extra five miles per hour on the fast ball after that! My dad played professional baseball, and he would never miss one of our baseball games for any money in the world, just like I wouldn't miss one of my kid's games. A client could call me up right now and say, "I've got a million dollar deal, but you're not going to get it unless you come now." If one of my kids had a baseball game, football game, or basketball game, I'd say, "Your million bucks and you will stay put until I take care of the most important thing in my life today, which is my kid."

I have lived my life, and I have minimized my income because of that attitude. I'm here to tell you now—not being a wealthy man except by certain definitions of wealth—I know I have enough.

I like myself because I never put my family on the altar. I really like and love my parents because they never put us on the altar of money.

You can't achieve balance until you have first established the foundation of *enough*. In order to establish this foundation, you have to set the parameters for what is enough in your life, your house, your car, where you vacation, what you spend your money on, and so forth.

For example, I might need a $15,000 Rolex, whereas somebody else only needs a $25 Timex because all he needs to know is what time it is and isn't trying to impress anybody. We really have to ask ourselves why we choose to wear a $15,000 Rolex instead of a $25 Timex. The time is the same, as I understand. If I look at my watch now, it's 5 o'clock regardless of whether I'm looking at my Timex or my Rolex, so the issue of which watch to buy comes down to whom I'm trying to impress. We're trying to impress others and ourselves.

Once you've got balance and a parameter for your needs, the next step is, more importantly than anything else, to not take yourself too seriously. If you don't take yourself too seriously, you'll be okay with the Timex. Of course, if you're a giver, and you're giving God his dime on the dollar, and you're taking care of your family, and you can afford a Rolex, go get it if you want it., because you've got balance. You've got enough. You probably don't take yourself seriously.

I drive a nice car–an Audi. I could drive a Corolla, but I'd rather drive an Audi because I can afford an Audi and I worked hard to get to that place. This is where you can't beat yourself up, especially because this is where religion can beat you up. In the same way that religion can't help you in setting these parameters, advertising also constantly beats you with the lie that you're not amounting to what you should. Advertisements tell you that you're not really the man, you're not really the woman, you're not really anybody unless you look this way, dress that way, possess this, and so forth.

Unless you have your parameters established, you won't know where your balancing act needs to be and where it begins. You will always try to react to that imposed feeling of inadequacy because you never sat down to say what the clear parameters are for your needs.

For example, I see those guys on the ab-machines with arms the size of my thighs. Though I'm a pretty big guy, I compare myself to them. They've got a double six pack and I've got a keg, but I look at them and think, if I'm going to look at my adequacy and self-respect based on these guys, I'm in big trouble.

I can't judge my adequacy and self-respect as a man based on whether I can afford that Porsche or that Benz or that Bentley. When you keep moving up the ladder, you just keep moving up the ladder.

When I was 25, my Firebird 400, which was worth about five grand at the time, was tremendous. It was a great car, but no matter how great the car, as you grow older and make more money, you will tend to keep buying and pursuing that "higher" standard or that perception that you can't yet afford. Then you make more money and suddenly, you look around and you're living in *this* neighborhood. Then ten years later, you're suddenly living in *this* neighborhood, driving this car, and hanging out in places that are different from the places in which you used to hang out before.

During my childhood, my family would go out to dinner at Denny's, a coffee shop chain all over the United States. That was eating out for us. My wife and I are lucky because we are privileged enough to be able to go to Cheesecake Factory or PF Chang's the way my parents used to take us out to Denny's. We've been blessed with education and experience. Despite those blessings, advertisements will always attack our sense of 'enough.' Advertisements attack our sense of self-worth and adequacy because they constantly compare us to other people.

How does religion respond to this? If you talk to most people across the board who go to whatever church or temple, they'll tell you that by and large, if one guy drives to church in a Porsche and another guy drives up in a beat-up station wagon, there will be immediate prejudices directed toward both of those people. Jesus, however, had a beautiful parable that speaks to this. In the parable, a widow comes to the treasury of the temple, where the Pharisees and religious leaders are standing around. The widow shows up and drops a few pennies, if you will, in the offering plate. Jesus says, "You see that widow? That lady has given more than these other people who have thrown in hundreds of times as much money because she gave out of her lack and out of her love for God and obedience, as opposed to giving out of her excess."

We should never care about prejudging someone, whether he drives a Porsche or a beat-up station wagon. That person in the station wagon may make 50 grand a year and may give two grand to the church. The guy in the Porsche could be making five hundred thousand, and he could treat God like a bellhop. That guy might throw a hundred bucks in the till and act like he's doing God a favor. The bottom line is the heart. Everything is in the heart.

No one can simply sit and look at people and figure out where exactly their hearts are. The only way we can know about people is by what fruits they bear and manifest in their lives. It is useless to be super religious without having a great foundation with God.

People who have a solid relationship with God could give a diddly doo dang whether a guy drives a Porsche or a beat-up station wagon. Those people know that a car's worth is not important. They don't care; they're not impressed. What's impressive is what kind of fruit a person bears. How does he treat his kids? Does he make time for his kids or does he make a million dollars but never see them?

I've heard stories of religious leaders making millions of dollars a year in south Orange County, religious leaders who never go to their kids' functions and send their kids' bodyguards to the events instead. Let's say that this person's relationship with God is right. Let's say that he realizes that, by and large, he's a horse's ass and God provided him the salvation and he accepts that he can't work his way into it. Okay, so he goes to heaven, but because of what God did, not what he did. Then there is the issue of fellowship. A proper, working, functioning fellowship with God provides the vertical line for how to treat your family, your friends, and each other. If the guy in the example ignores this vertical line, I have to think that during this guy's life, God will let him know. God will always let His kids know where they're out of line. Sometimes, he gets our attention through a knock on the door from the process service saying your wife is leaving you. That'll wake you up. Or your kid says, "I'm moving out," "I'm pregnant," or "I'm on drugs." God will get your attention somehow.

Your appearance of being a righteous, church-going, wonderful person in the eyes of the religious community can be the illusion. But the reality that you are actually screwed up in the context of what God has called you to do and who God called you to love is something from which you can't hide. Even if you're a pastor or leader of a church, your church's needs should not take precedence over your family's. The number one priority that God has given us to take care of is our family. They're number one, above yourself, above your job, and above your friends. If you aren't married, your family is with your mom and your dad in the meantime. Take care of your parents. Then take care of your friends, your extended family and the people at your church or temple. You are a lover, a giver, and a caretaker. When you transition into the time when God brings that right person across your path, your priorities will also transition.

When scripture says, "For this cause, a man shall leave his mother and father and cleave unto his wife," it draws attention to this new priority. This scripture doesn't mean that my wife and I are going to be the same person, think the same way, and never get into conflicts. Marriage just changes priorities. What God calls us to do in maintaining balance between our work and home is to shift our priorities. Unfortunately, we are constantly trying to shift our priorities to overcome religious prejudices or religious preconceived notions. Then, we're fighting advertisements and the world's competitiveness, also called "keeping up with the Joneses."

When we try to combat these things without God's Word, we can't do it. Unless we know what God has to say about something and we're obedient to it, we're never truly in God's economy or in relationship with God. Without the Word, we will never learn true north, or the concept of "enough," and "enough" is exactly what we need to understand before we can achieve any balance between work and home.

Chapter 8: Friendship
and Community in the Digital Age

Relationships thrive on communication and they die because of miscommunication. Today's social media outlets are what I call *inadequate* communication. These outlets may not represent *mis*communication, but relying on social media to sustain healthy communities is not enough.

The paradox of the digital age is that these communication tools actually drag down our ability to communicate with each other, and in turn, drag down our ability to communicate with and have a relationship with God. On the flip side, an active, communicative relationship with God can help us nurture successful relationships with our families, friends, and business associates.

The problem with technology is that what is meant to be a fantastic communication tool can be misused and abused to our detriment. Research indicates that even texting transforms the way people think. Because text messages lack the adverbial clauses or the complexity of thought we find in a traditional sentence, young people who use texting as a primary means of communication don't develop the ability to communicate deeply with others.

If texting can become a problem in our children, why do parents give their kids cell phone privileges? Today, even eight-year-olds have access to cell phones because we want to know where our kids are. Your kid is at a party at Suzie's house, and you want to call to say, "Are you okay? When can I pick you up?" or you want your kid to have the freedom to call you from the party to say, "I'm not happy. I want to come home early." Your teenagers have cell phones in case the car breaks down. Parents want to know where their kids are. Parents want security, and they're willing to do what it takes to get it, barring putting a GPS ankle bracelet on their kids.

Those of us who grew up in the '60s and '70s didn't have cell phones, but on the other hand, I remember times when my car broke down, forcing me to drive into an unsafe part of town and hope to God that I wouldn't get mugged while I hunted a payphone to ask my dad for help!

The Internet is another example of an important tool that can be manipulated to harm us. The Internet speeds up communication and provides endless information, but it also comes with pornography and scams, and gives both kids and adults a completely false slant on the reality of the world.

The problem with liberty is that it can be warped to constrain us. The Internet and television and other technologies can be used as blessings, educational tools, and social enhancements, but they can also become tools of bondage, tools of miscommunication, and tools of corrupt values. In order to make sure these communication tools are used for productive purposes, parents must communicate effectively with their kids. They must become enmeshed in this need for communication even when the kids don't want to communicate because they see their friends texting *their* parents. Parents must establish ground rules such as "no phones at the kitchen table" or "no phones at the restaurant." This boils down to an issue of courage. Parents need to resist the urge to let cell phones and other gadgets baby-sit their kids. Five to ten years ago, parents were fighting Game Boys. Fifteen years ago, it was VCRs, and when I was growing up, my parents probably sat me in front of Foghorn Leghorn cartoons.

When we let technology consume our lives, we aren't able to develop our communication skills. We become limited in our ability to articulate creatively. If you talk to kids under 25 years old, you'll find that many of them lack greatly in the communication department. The exceptions to the rule seem to be the readers, but the problem is that we have a society of kids who are not readers. The psychologist may say, "Well, there's too much sugar in the cereal so they're all ADD and can't sit still to read," but I don't believe this is the case.

Parents must be creative enough to read to their kids while they're young and find ways to engage their more complex thoughts and language abilities. Find books on tape and play them when the family takes a car trip. You could put in one of the classics—Mark Twain's *Huckleberry Finn*, for example—and let the kids listen to that and exercise their imagination instead of sitting there engrossed in a Game Boy.

Platforms such as LinkedIn and Facebook that help us connect with people also become distractions away from our immediate lives. I can't tell you how many times I get notices saying, "So-and-so wants you to join LinkedIn" and "So-and-so wants you to be a friend on MySpace." People tell me I have to have a Facebook page for my business now that I'm an author, and that's probably true, but too much of a good thing can be a distraction.

My sons, ages 27, 25, 23, and 18, are knee-deep in social media, but personally, these mediums cause me to be unproductive. Don't get me wrong, I use the technology. I've got an iPhone— I happen to have the type of business that requires a lot of email communication with clients—but for the most part, I've avoided whatever is unnecessary beyond required communication.

A specific example of the way social media can distract is the danger of an old high school boyfriend or girlfriend finding you forty years later because he or she has searched for your MySpace or Facebook page to find out who you are now and where you are. You get a message on your Facebook wall. The next thing you know, there's a reunion, followed by fantasies of "We were in love at 18 so this certainly makes sense at 60." No, it doesn't. There's a reason why you broke up with this person at 18, and there are probably plenty more reasons why you would at 60. The point is that social media will sometimes circumvent what you've got going on in your life right now if you're unable to confront, communicate, correct, and love the people who are already present. The irony today is that we've got all these technological devices that permit communication instantaneously, but we have less real communication today with loved ones, with friends, and with anyone than ever before. Although everybody talks about the so-called online "community," those virtual spaces such as LinkedIn and Facebook become temptations away from genuine community. At my age, I haven't been lured by the Facebook and MySpace deal mostly because I don't have time to be distracted by them. Today, between text messages and emails and various social media platforms, most of us don't have the discipline to sit down and say, "I'll check these in the morning and before I leave work, but during the middle of the day, I've got things to do and I can't be distracted." When we hear the old email ding, we have a tendency to go straight to the culprit, or our cell phone constantly vibrates because of text messages.

If you discipline yourself in regard to the media and your technological devices, you'll become more peaceful as you gain control of your life. Instead of responding to every ding, beep, or buzz that comes your way, it's important to establish the priority of a sense of urgency. Set up a system with your spouse, for example, in case of emergencies. Call rather than text, or send a text that says that the next call will be important. Prioritizing what you respond to and what you can afford to put on hold will increase a positive flow of communication to the people who are important to you.

Research also indicates that the older generation—the plus-40 generation— hasn't lost the ability to communicate as much as the younger, under-30 generation has. The under-30 crowd hardly makes phone calls anymore. They text. Writing letters is unheard of. In the old days, if you wanted intimate communication, you would write a physical letter. When computers arrived, you could type out the letter, personally sign it, then hand it to somebody in an envelope. With the Internet, you send it as an attachment and hope that the feeling you want to convey will transfer through email. I joke with my wife all the time that if she could function with me 90% of the time by texting to say, "Dinner's ready," she'd do it!

Sometimes, the preference for certain modes of communication comes from a personality difference as opposed to a generational gap. For example, I've found that Type A people prefer phone calls to text messages. I'm a Type A person, and when I get a text from somebody, I hit the call button and ask, "What do you want?" When my buddies want to talk about the Angels or the Dodgers, I don't want to punch numbers, misspell all my words, and look like a blubbering idiot. I want to *talk*. I want to hear a voice on the other line!

I need the intimacy of a voice. I want the fully fleshed out conversation. People with Type B personalities could care less whether they ever talk to anybody on the phone. They seem to be happy with "How are you?" to which they text back, "Great." This could be a function of Type B personalities being more passive, not having much to say, and not wanting to tell stories.

I love to tell stories! You can't tell a story via text. Stories must be told when others can hear you so that you can soak up every reaction, hear them laugh, hear them snort... hear them tell you to shut up.

In the same vein, I'm sure the telephone was a pain for people back in the 1910s. They got tired of the phone ringing the way I get tired of texts. So the problem appears not to be with the media, but with *us*. Who knows? In a hundred years, we might telepathically send messages to people like in that Mel Gibson film, *What Women Want*, where he knew exactly what women wanted by reading their minds.

The problem with our lack of community and the way it affects our spirituality has less to do with technology and more to do with the way we allow technology to distract us from what we need to do to communicate in an effective manner to our loved ones or to our business associates. Instead of enhancing our ability to communicate, technology comes with a thousand new rules that tell us to be careful not to offend somebody. Don't underline. Don't highlight. Don't make it bold. Don't do this. Don't do that.

When I speak to somebody, they know whether a word was bold or not. They know whether I've used an exclamation point or a question mark. Typing sometimes leaves too much room for miscommunication. How many times have you written an email—personal or business—that conveyed the exact opposite message of what you intended to get across? Then when that person is mad at you or passive-aggressive towards you and you don't know why, you are affected spiritually. Miscommunication causes doubt, confusion, and anger. When I send somebody a message, I expect a response. When I don't get an appropriate response, I become angry, and my anger affects my spiritual peace.

Effective spiritual leaders help ground us before we let these media outlets affect us negatively. Most pastors don't wake up in the morning and think, "How can I give an ineffective sermon?" but addressing the issues of the digital age requires a lot of honesty, and the willingness to say what people don't want to hear. People like to embrace what's popular. They don't want to hear about how those popular things can be harmful.

Rabbis, pastors, priests, and other spiritual shepherds need to be aware of the temptations that exist in social media and technology. They need to know how to communicate those dangers and then steer the conversation back to the primary foundation of spirituality—our relationship with God. If you're communicating effectively with God, chances are you will communicate effectively with your spouse, your kids, and your business associates as well.

As we've said before, we must first establish and accept our relationship with God based on what He did, then move horizontally to figure out how to love Him in return and also how to love others. We have to return to the foundational message of the Golden Rule. To apply the basic premise of the Golden Rule in this context, we have to ask, "How would I like to be communicated to?" and then communicate with others accordingly.

Most people who lack great relationships with God don't communicate regularly with Him. Then, because they don't access His scriptures to understand what God's intention and will is for their lives, they also feel that God doesn't communicate with them.

Leaders in the church, synagogue or mosque should preach messages of effective communication. They should emphasize that communication is a two-way street. Communication must be received and understood in order to be effective. Someone might hear or see your words, but those words might be misinterpreted and cause a breach in communication because that person can't figure out what you mean in a short text or can't understand what you meant by your few bold words and underlined phrases. Before we set out to communicate with others, we must do a little homework to find out how they receive communication. Ask your spouse. Ask your kids. Ask your friends.

Oftentimes, family members will forward email jokes to you instead of paragraphs with actual content about their lives, or they'll send slams on the President, and they think they're communicating. That's not what my wife and I want from our family. We want a genuine "How are you?" I'd prefer a simple paragraph explaining how you are, rather than a joke. Communication requires an ebb and a flow, a give and a take.

I have a 23-year-old son who is a brilliant kid with a Type B personality. He spends almost five hours a day gaming, and is not a communicator. If you talk to my son, you'll find that he's a fantastic speaker who reads a lot and actually has written a couple of books himself, but he could care less about sitting down with people and talking. That kind of communication doesn't motivate him.

If you have a personality similar to my son's, how will this affect your communication with God and your spiritual development? If direct, verbal communication isn't your forte, there's no reason why you can't text God or email God. I've even told my sons that they could write letters to God. I've told them that they need to quit trying to formulate the right words that they think God wants to hear. "Religion" tells us that we need to pray this way or that—that we have to say "In Jesus' name" at the end of the prayer or say the Hail Mary an x number of times in order for God to hear us and not put us on hold.

Many people have asked me how to pray. The disciples of Jesus Christ also asked him to teach them to pray, and he broke it down. Jesus said, first of all, to acknowledge God for who He is: "You're a mighty God, and I'm not." Proclaim what God has done. He has established a kingdom here on earth called the kingdom of heaven. ' Thy kingdom come, thy will (or intention) be done."

Jesus talked about provision. He said that we should ask God to give us "our daily bread," which means our daily provision, our daily sales, our daily health, or whatever it is we need. We say to God, "I know that you're the giver and provider of good things."

In addition to being the provider, God has many names in Jewish scripture: Jehovah the provider, Jehovah the refuge, Jehovah the healer, the shield. The Hebrews had countless names for God, which our generation has forgotten.

In prayer, we acknowledge who God is, and who we're not. Then we ask God to keep us from temptation. Write your temptations down and tear them up!

I recently had a conversation with my 25-year-old son Nolan, who just graduated college, found that jobs are tight, and said, "I don't know where to start." I said, first of all, start with who you are in God. You're his kid. You're royalty. You're important. You're in the kingdom *now*, on earth.

In everything, we have to ground ourselves in who God is and who we are in God. If we do this, we won't communicate abusively. We'll communicate effectively because we are secure in our identities. People who know who they are and have confidence because of who they are in God communicate in a loving—and when necessary, an effective, correcting and disciplinary—fashion. Ineffective communication is the equivalent of ignoring our most important relationships—our spouses and our kids—and not calling them when we have something important to say, but texting them their "Happy Birthday."

Say you've offended your wife and she's upstairs, upset because of something you said, and instead of walking up there and hugging her and taking your lumps, you text, "I'm sorry, good night" because you want to avoid confrontation. In the meantime, your wife just wants to vent and be held. How effective is it to let your insecurities interfere with your communications?

We need to establish, build, and sustain relationships, not run from them. We do this by establishing, building, and sustaining our relationship with God.

God often talks about the spoken word. He tells us to profess with our mouths what He said in the word so that we hear it and the people around us hear it so that there is no doubt that this is what we believe. This includes professing and claiming the identities God gives us—the words God says about me being His beloved kid.

In my prayer closet, in my prayers to God, I talk loudly not only because I want to hear it, but also because I want the enemy to hear it. I want the enemy to hear me proclaim what God has to say about me and my situation and what He's done about it and what He'll do about it. God, in so many words, will say, "If you'll trust me, if you'll dwell in me, and if you'll follow my commandments so we can have that functional, productive fellowship, I will rebuke the 'devourer' for your sake."

God says, "I will kick ass and take names on your behalf."

So, in order to communicate with God, we can use the Lord's Prayer as a foundation. Begin with who God is, what He's established, what we need, and end it with the glorious proclamation: "For thine is the kingdom, and the power and glory forever. Amen."

If prayer doesn't come naturally and it's easier for you to focus by using the media and technology available, do it. We have methods of communication that didn't exist 50 years ago. We talked about the ways that these methods can harm us, but we also need to use these tools to enhance our communication not only with each other, but also with God. Why not sit at your computer and type a message to God? This especially relates to the way our kids communicate. As parents, you've got to be creative with them and suggest, "Get on the computer and write God a letter."

Adults can take advantage of this, too. Get on the computer and write, "Dear God, these are the ten things I'd like to see happen in my life." Get on the computer and say, at 40 years old and laid off from your company, what kind of job you want or where you want to live. Let God know.

In the Old City of Jerusalem, you can find the Western Wall, or the Wailing Wall, which is the last remaining piece of the second temple, which was destroyed by the Romans in 70 A.D. Similar to the idea of typing a letter to God, the tradition of the Wailing Wall is that visitors—Jews and non-Jews alike—write a little note to God and stick it in the wall.

When we write letters to God, we must expect to hear an answer. Since we know that communication is a two-way street, we should not only communicate to God, but also expect that He will speak in return. Instead of saying, "Dear God, thanks a lot for the mess I'm in," begin with "Dear God, you are a mighty God."

Then say, "I am lucky you love me. I want to please you. I want to be protected by your angels and win the daily war against the enemy. More importantly, I want to function in this fellowship with you effectively. I love you. Signed, Congregant."

God doesn't respond to our needs. God responds to us acknowledging who He is and who we are in Him—His children. He responds to us understanding the fact that He is our rewarder and the solver of the problems we bring before Him.

God speaks in a variety of ways. He's already written a pretty good book—the Bible, a bestseller. We dismiss it by saying it's not relevant to us today, but the book *is* relevant as long as humans still have beating hearts. Humans are imperfect and we need a savior to rescue us from ourselves and from each other. The Bible addresses this need, and also tells the stories of countless people who have maintained active, effective communication with God.

Communication is the heart of great relationships—great community—with people and with God. In today's digital age, our most popular communication tools such as text messages and Facebook often harm our brain's ability to maintain meaningful contact with others.

We have to guard against this vigilantly. Churches and synagogues don't teach us about the ways we fail to communicate with each other and with God because they still operate out of the old model, which claims that our brains are well-fitted to relate to God. We see now that our brains have actually been well-fitted only by a world system that promotes the self and not God.

If we want to pursue great relationships with God, we must, in a manner of speaking, wash our brains with God's word. We've certainly been inundated with ads, marketing avenues, and the enemy's lies, so we must wash our minds with truth.

Imagine your brain is a car with a gunked-up carburetor that needs to be cleaned to function properly, or perhaps your fuel injections need to be unclogged in order for the machine to run efficiently. We can de-gunk by constantly reading God's word and hearing God's word at our respective churches or synagogues or mosques. When we ignore God's word and stop communicating with God, we feel the gunk of the world begin to take the performance of our engines down several notches.

In this digital age, we must cleanse our minds of the constant distractions in our paths in order to run our lives efficiently. Only then can we build healthy, lasting relationships with our communities and with God.

CHAPTER 9: ACCOUNTABILITY

The relationship that can serve as the crux through which God deals with us, strengthens us, loves us, hugs us, and heals us is our relationship with what I call our *accountability group*. I was first introduced to the concept of an accountability group around the age of 45, and it has been one of the greatest blessings in my life. In my case, my accountability group is a group of men whom I trust. Accountability groups are often comprised of the people we call "true friends"—friends who know the ins and outs of who we are and love us in spite of them.

When I think of what a friend really is, I recall the sermons of a wonderful minister, G. Campbell Morgan, who preached in London in the late 1800s into the early 1900s. G. Campbell Morgan was a simple, powerful speaker who led many revivals in London and preached about being "God's friend."

God designed us and created us. He knows our deepest secrets—what makes us tick and what breaks us—yet He loves us exceedingly in spite of our carnality or our sinful, rebellious nature. God chooses to be our friend in our darkest, most unattractive moments. Accountability comes from *this* concept of friendship.

The underlying message of this book has been that our first relationship—our primary accountability session—must be with God. We need to break down our religious barriers to understand that God establishes relationship with us as a gift. We don't earn it. It's not forced upon us. It is a free gift. When we accept this gift of relationship with God, we begin to work to understand what that relationship entails so that functional, fruitful fellowship, as we've called it, will ensue. As we've mentioned before, this relationship relies on our understanding of who God is and who we are in God. We study God's word to figure out what God wants for us so that we're the most effective, most at peace, and most ready to fight the war against the enemy, the devil. The better we understand God's word, the better we can throw those truths back in evil's face when it confronts us in life.

Much of this battle relates to our identity. If your true identity is wrapped up in God, in who God says you are, what he has for you, and what your assignment is, and not in what you do or accomplish or what you make in terms of money or products, then you are better equipped to face your battles.

An accountability group, then, consists of the people around you who can constantly remind you of your true identity and hold you accountable to that identity.

I've found that the people whom I consider successful in life are the ones who understand their identity in God. They understand that they're God's children who are special–royalty. They understand that they've been given their allotted time on earth to affect and influence people for the kingdom of the heavens and the eternal life that we're living now.

Once you operate out of that knowledge of your true identity in God, you will then be able to say, "I can love others as I want to be loved because I know how I want to be loved because of who I am in God and how well God loves me." When you acknowledge and accept who you are in God and what God has done for you, then his nature—his nature of love, his nature of joy, his nature of peace, his nature of patience—will become your second nature. What Christians call the "fruits of the Spirit," found in Galatians chapter 5, will begin to manifest in your life. Then you will begin to have faith in God and stop depending on faith in yourself.

Accountability is having people around you who will lovingly remind you of who you are in God. These people won't blow sunshine up your hindsight. [What does this mean?] They won't lie to you or flatter you for their own purposes. They will be concerned with *your* identity in God, which means that they better be people who know who *they* are in God so that they're not ineffective accountability mates. An accountability group, then, is a group of like-minded people who understand who they are in God and know how special they are so that they're able to love you, protect you, and not gossip with the information you give them. They exist to help you continue to be the best spouse, parent, friend, businessperson and member of your community.

Over the last 20 years, I've found people in my life—former pastors, best friends, my wife and even my sons—who have held me accountable. My sons, who know that I know God and love God, will often say, "Dad, remember what you told us about this" or "Dad, remember who you are in God" because sometimes, I might want to respond to situations in ways that God does not want me to respond when I feel slighted, violated, or disrespected.

Also over the last 20 years, I've gotten together regularly with four or five guys for what we call our communion night. This is my accountability group, which looks different from the Christian norm. Our communion night consists of a fine bottle of wine, cigars out on the patio, and conversations about God and life.

Some people might get stuck on the *do dos* and *don't don'ts* of religion and say, "Hey, you're smoking a cigar. That's a sin," or "You're drinking wine. That's a sin." Jesus didn't change water into Kool-Aid, and I am aware that the scriptures constantly warn against drinking wine in excess so that we'll avoid making bad decisions.

I don't have a drinking problem, not because of religion, but because of the stability of my understanding of who I am in God. When you drink in excess, you begin to make decisions outside of your true identity. You make bad decisions sexually, financially, and you say the wrong things relationally.

Because of who I am in God, I act as God's ambassador. I don't want to embarrass God. God doesn't come down to hug people; He has me hug them. God doesn't come down and talk to somebody about his problems; God has me do it. God uses people who are secure in their identity in Him and people who make themselves available to help others.

In addition to understanding your identity in God, your accountability group must love God and be trustworthy. Trustworthiness is the key to proper accountability. The kind of trustworthiness you need in an accountability group that is real, authentic, and godly goes beyond what a counselor or therapist can do for a hundred bucks an hour. You must trust your accountability partners with your life and secrets, along with your warts, sins and bad habits. You trust that they care about your best and love you in spite of those warts, sins and bad habits.

In that genuine accountability group, you invite the Holy Spirit to come in the midst of that group to say, "I have some solutions for you" as you look for answers in God's word for any problems you're fighting through. The Holy

Spirit grants us the wisdom we need in all situations, and as Proverbs says, that wisdom often comes from having "a multitude of counselors."

We can never be wise in and of ourselves. We threaten the enemy the most when two or more of us are gathered to seek God. The serpent came into the Garden of Eden because he saw that with one person he had no problems, but with two, he had big problems. The serpent schemed in order to disrupt the fellowship between the man, the woman, and God.

Ecclesiastes 4:12 says, "Though one may be overpowered, two can defend themselves. A cord of three strands is not quickly broken." The scriptures continually say that it's important to have people around us who can lift us up. Even Moses needed Aaron to lift him up, help him, and assist him because he became weary. Elijah needed Elisha. Jesus also had his top two or three, probably Peter and John, to help him do what he needed to do, both spiritually and emotionally.

The devil attacks any union designed to strengthen people as each other's helpmates, friends, counselors, prayer partners, and so forth. The devil attacks marriages and friendships to weaken that cord of three strands. A godly friendship between a few guys or a couple of women is a huge threat to the devil so he will do whatever he can to lie, steal, and cheat in that relationship through gossip and hurt feelings. In order to fight the devil's lies, your strength must be rooted in knowing who you are in God first.

In an accountability group, you're not necessarily asking for advice or solutions to your problems. You're being held accountable to your true self in God. People don't have solutions for you. Only God has solutions, so your accountability partners' job is to be people who point you to God so that you can implement God's solutions. This is why, when I have problems, I feel a strong need to get away with my buds, talk it out, hug it out, cry it out, or do whatever it is we need to do. I'm relying on them to redirect me to God.

Through that accountability group, I know I have people lifting me up in prayer, and as these people intercede for me before God, I gain the confidence and strength to face my battles and emerge victorious. An accountability group will only be successful if the people involved constantly say, "I know you may have a problem, but you are God's beloved child, and we serve a mighty God."

Various religious institutions understand the power of community, but instead of advocating for accountability groups with this purpose, they will often promote groups that look more like social clubs. Churches call these "small groups."

Small groups can be productive, but men should be grouped with men, and women with women. Many religious leaders will tell you that your spouse has to be your best friend, but I can tell you for a fact that I can say things to my buddies about something I'm going through that I can't say to my wife. As kings of God-given domains, men must protect their wives, who are the helpmates and support. If you're dealing with drinking or sexual temptation or working through a problem with your spouse, then you should look to yourself first before looking at your spouse. Examine *your* problems in the relationship and *your* lack of communication. Instead of worrying your spouse when you're just going through small issues that everybody goes through, look to your accountability group as a safe, confidential environment where you can begin to make discoveries about yourself.

A lot of people go to counselors to work out the kinks in their lives.[58] But again, a productive accountability group will know you better and redirect you to who *you* really are because they'll know you in an authentic way. Your group will tell you, "It sounds like a bad idea to present your issue to your wife this way. Have you considered this?" or "That's not a good way to approach your kid. Have you considered this?" An accountability group will ask how you are forgetting who you are in God and how that is negatively affecting your marriage or whatever relationship you're struggling with. The group is a chance to test out your solutions in a safe environment that will promote God's wisdom to come forth.

Although this type of accountability may not be specifically mandated by God, I like to call it a "Randyism." The Randyism here is this: I believe that there are certain topics that you should bring to someone you can trust in an accountability capacity in order to make sure that the decisions you make are ones that will love and serve your spouse. When you struggle with sexual issues—not necessarily issues of infidelity, but problems regarding the intimacy between you and your spouse—you should be able to go to your accountability group. Sometimes, approaching your spouse first will only mean a verbal slap in the face and no sex for another two months!

Whether the issue is a need for your sexual desires for each other to be rekindled or the challenge of the lack of spontaneity in your marriage, your accountability group will be a group of godly people who understand who they are and understand their responsibility before God to be truthful and authentic while directing their advice through the filter of God's word.

This ties in with the reason why same-gender small groups work better than couples' small groups or "Couples' Bible Study." You can't waltz into a room of five to seven couples, sit down, and announce, "George and I are having problems in bed." In a couples' group, you won't know whether everybody in the group is on the same page regarding accountability guidelines. Does each person in that room have a firm grasp on who he or she is in God? Do you know that each person is trustworthy? Will the group give you advice filtered through God's word because the people in the group love you? My church will oftentimes host a men's breakfast. Sometimes, forty guys will show up to this breakfast on a Saturday morning. This is not the place to go to ask, "Does anybody have a problem we can pray about?" or to say, "I've got a problem. I haven't been laid for two years in my marriage." Whether you've got intimacy issues with your spouse or you're on the verge of bankruptcy, a small group or church function—co-ed or not—is not the place to air this kind of personal business. Productive accountability comes from an understanding of who you are in God and a deep understanding of who the others in the accountability group are in God.

Similarly, the success of Alcoholics Anonymous and Al-Anon comes from the participants' understanding that there's a distinction between what you share with your sponsor or your mentor versus what you share with the larger group. In any twelve-step program, you reserve the intimate details for your sponsor or mentor, and share only general information at the group level. Spilling every intimate detail to the larger group is inappropriate and also selfish because you end up taking the group hostage to listen to your problems. Conversely, the group will have little to offer you in terms of productive advice.

Churches and synagogues are great for the purpose of being fed by God's word, but regarding accountability, religious functions— be they fellowship outreaches or small groups—will fall short when you need those intimate conversations that work through your deepest issues. Fellowship outreaches, like social clubs, typically ask, "What are this group's needs?", and then respond by creating a divorce recovery workshop or a singles group that is simply a safe place for singles to meet other singles. These groups shouldn't be sugar coated to pretend to be something different or something more spiritual. The word of God is not designed to segregate people into specific groups and say, "The Holy Spirit will minister to us alone because we're singles 25 to 35 who don't want any overweight or unattractive people in our group." These groups—singles bowling on Saturday mornings or couples' hiking trips—are great opportunities to meet people and have fun, but they are ineffective means for the more intimate work of the Holy Spirit.

The basic function of the church is to feed, equip, and provide people with the word of God. The church should establish the members of its congregation in their true identities in God and constantly remind them of the importance of their primary relationship with God. What a church *community* looks like and how that community should behave will look different depending on political, social, and cultural circumstances. A church in Uganda looks different from a church in Afghanistan. The church in the first century, when the Jews were in violation of Roman authorities by breaking off and forming The Way instead of acknowledging Caesar as the divine head, will look different from an American church today because that first church was in survival mode and was filled with constant tension.

Compare that first church of the book of Acts to the church community in south Orange County and you'll find vastly different needs. Telling church members in south Orange County to sell all their possessions to give to the poor will accomplish very little. The church in south Orange County or in the United States by and large is not suffering from lack of money or constant economic devastation to the extent that the only solution would be to create a socialistic economy like the Acts church, where everyone puts money into a pot to make sure everyone has enough to eat and homes to live in.

Church communities vary depending on locale. Similarly, accountability groups differ depending on the people in the accountability group. Your group will be specifically designed to fit your needs and the needs of those people you trust.

Of course, although the *way* someone preaches might be different, God remains the same. How a church functions or meets or serves is mandated by the political and cultural restraints and freedoms of its locale, but the word of God and God's character are the same message of love no matter what time period you're in or where you go.

In order to let the truths of God and God's purposes for a group, whether a large church or an accountability group of four men, prevail, we have to let the rules of God supersede the rules of men. This requires wisdom, and luckily, the Holy Spirit is in the wisdom business. The Holy Spirit directs us and tells us what our individual communities should look like. The Holy Spirit will tell you what your accountability group will look like, and will tell you in what context it is okay or not okay to share your individual problems.

The bottom line of all communities, however, is this: "Where two or three come together in my name, there I am with them" (Matthew 18:30). When I get together with a small group of people who trust the word of God, I know that we can invite God to be in our midst and access what he means when he says, "I'm in the healing business, and I'll do what any two of you who've come together ask for in my name."

Large crusades or large groups are productive when somebody in the audience hears God's word and responds to it, but if that person doesn't find an accountability group, he or she will lose that important feeling of belonging. An accountability group will love you, hold you accountable to what God's word says, remind you of your true identity, and then challenge you when you believe the enemy's lies about your given situations.

We all have a tendency to fall into insecurities and lies regarding our identity. When we find ourselves saying, "I'm never going to amount to anything" or "I'll never find a job" or "I'm never going to beat this drinking problem," our accountability partners must be the ones to slap us across the face, figuratively, like Cher slapping Nicholas Cage in *Moonstruck*, and demand, "Snap out of it!"

Your accountability group is more than a social gathering of friends. It is more than a couple of beers with the guys or miniature golfing with the girls. The trustworthy, loving people in your accountability group are the ones who remind you of your truest identity in God when you, like everybody else, struggle to remind yourself.

CHAPTER 10: STEWARDSHIP
AND SERVICE, SOWING AND REAPING

Giving is at the heart of our financial management. In fact, giving is also at the heart of our personal management, our relationship management and work management.

The heart of God is the heart of a giver. If you have the spirit of God within you—if you fully understand the God-Father relationship—the fruits of that spirit will manifest in the ways you give of your finances, your time and your giftedness.

This chapter strikes an important chord for me because it is in conversation with my book, *The Safe Money System*, which evolved from a culmination of thirty years in the financial services counseling people regarding money. That book focuses on our relationship with money, and this chapter will put that relationship within the deeper context of scripture.

Let's begin with one of my favorite proverbs regarding financial stewardship. Proverbs 11:24-25 says, "One man gives freely, yet gains even more; another withholds unduly and comes to poverty. A generous man will prosper; he who refreshes others will himself be refreshed." It is important to keep in mind that this proverb was written by not only one of the wisest men of all time, but also one of the richest—King Solomon of Israel.

As we dig into this proverb, we see that the main element is incredibly powerful. This proverb challenges us to imagine an individual who is so generous that he refreshes others, and yet is refreshed by his own generosity! It is when this person begins to give that somehow his giving returns to him.

One of the greatest events of my life was my transition from being a stockbroker, what I call a "bookie," to being a true retirement strategist and financial advisor dealing with safety and establishing relationships with people to help them achieve long term, successful financial security. I remember sitting out one night on a hill overlooking the El Toro Marine Base and watching the jets take off. That night, with my mind as clear as a bell, I reassessed my life. I thought, "I played baseball for eleven years and was a business major, and is this what my life is about? I'm going to be a bookie?" I admitted in that moment that I hated it. I didn't want to be in financial sales anymore. I was tired of the uncertainty, the risk and the bookie mentality.

Then I heard the life-changing voice of God say to me, very, very clearly,

"Randy, you will never be able to help my people unless you yourself have gone through it, understand it, and can teach them the right way to do it." That voice — that 'vision,' if you will — set my next 25 years into action.

Interestingly enough, those next 25 years were filled with much chaos. When we reach that turning point in our lives at which God clearly outlines in our spirit that this is the path to follow, all hell breaks loose. As we discussed in Chapter 2, "The Devil's War," the enemy knows our assignment and destiny. Once we realize our callings and begin to march in that direction, the enemy will do everything to discourage, distract, defeat, and steal our vision. The enemy wants nothing more than to destroy the fruit of the vision that God has given to us to be a blessing to other people. Doing this would then keep us from receiving blessings as well. As Proverbs says, if you bless, or refresh, others, you yourself will be refreshed.

Within five years of my vision, I was doing well in business, but I went through an unwelcome divorce followed by eight years of financial and emotional devastation while I was single. At the same time, I was able to maintain my clients and not lose their money, which in turn blessed me so that I could be a blessing to my sons, raise them, spend time with them, and be a co-parent with my ex-wife so that our boys' needs could be met. In spite of the chaos, these blessings came as a result of that vision and calling from God.

When I remarried in 1998, my new wife thought that stability came in the form of a paycheck and benefits in the corporate world. She didn't fully understand my calling to be a financial advisor to people. Then, within three years, she went through two job changes in a tech market that fell apart, and she came to understand and be confident in what I do and how I do it with "The Safe Money System." That system has sustained us and provided a comfortable lifestyle, while giving her the ability to work part-time in order to raise her son, who was five when we got married.

This life was born out of what God spoke to me in that original vision. He said that in order for me to help others, I would have to go through a series of financial challenges to better help and understand people and have empathy for them.

True enough, during that time, the economy of 1983 was tough. I had done well for the first couple of years, but by 1983, I was struggling. The stock market was at an all-time low relative to the 1930's, inflation adjusted. Business was hard to come by just like it is today in 2010.

In that situation, I remember God telling me to *give* and *sow* my way out of financial trouble.

I thought to myself, "That doesn't make any sense!" Then I began receiving scriptures regarding this very word. Numbers 23:19-20 says, "God is not a man, that he should lie, nor a son of man, that he should change his mind. Does he speak and then not act? Does he promise and not fulfill? I have received a command to bless; he has blessed, and I cannot change it."

If you have little money, giving that money away is the last thing you want to do. Cerebrally, it doesn't make sense to give your money to gain more. In order to understand this principle, you first have to establish God's faithfulness. This passage in Numbers, for example, clearly establishes God's resoluteness when he makes promises with us. God, unlike human beings, will not change his mind. Nothing we can do will keep God from fulfilling his promise to bless us as we bless others.

Once we understand and receive this knowledge with faith, we can then find scriptures such as the book of Malachi, in which God challenges His people. In Malachi 3:8, God says, "Will a man rob God? Yet you rob me." At first glance, this passage sounds harsh. When we invite the Holy Spirit to begin a conversation with us regarding this passage, we, like the people in this Malachi passage, can ask, "How do we rob you?"

God's answer is that we rob Him when we don't bring our tithes and offerings—one-tenth of what he has given us—back to Him. God has given us the ability and talent to work, to make money, and to take care of our families. One of the things God requires of us is the proper management of our money and the proper management of our emotional attachment to money.

God wants you to give Him a tenth of what you have so that He can use it to take care of the people who have taught you and fed you, and also so that money never gains mastery over you.

I've met many people who have giving hearts, but I've also met many people who treat God like a bellhop. These are the people who think they're doing God a favor by flipping a five dollar bill or two into the offering plate when it comes by, or they think they have a charitable spirit if they buy a couple boxes of cookies from a Girl Scout. The people who have the heart of God are givers who give even out of their lack. They are the ones who understand what John meant when he said, "For God so loved the world, he *gave* his son."

That's part one—stewardship and service in offering our tithes to God, giving as a means of sowing. Part two is this: God didn't give His son without expecting a harvest. This is the key to this chapter–the reaping.

When you give in order to be obedient to and in line with what God's word teaches, you have to expect a harvest. You have to expect a multitude on top of your seed. Unfortunately, people feel uncomfortable with this concept and say, "Well, I'm not going to give to receive." This mentality comes from religious formulas and religious interpretations that if I give a buck, I'll receive thirty or a hundred. That's not what's being taught here.

What God teaches is that if you're a generous person, you will also be cared for. You will find favor in God. God will make sure that people seek you out.

In Malachi, God says to bring all the tithes into the storehouse so that there will be meat and food and supplies in His house. Then He says, "Test me in this" to see whether He "will not open for you the windows of heaven and pour out for you such a blessing that there will not be room enough to receive it" (Malachi 3:10). That doesn't sound to me like the language of lack. It doesn't sound like God is saying, "Maybe it'll happen, maybe it won't." If the book of Numbers says that God is not a man who would lie or change His mind, and if Malachi says that God will pour out too many blessings to contain, then giving your tithes becomes simple as long as you have faith that these scriptures speak truth.

It's not God's will for the teachers of scripture—for the church—to have financial lack. God required the nation of Israel to give one-tenth of its harvest, produce, and productivity to the Levites. The Levites were the priests who took care of the temple and performed all the activities of the priestly tribe.

Today, many people have a problem with saying that God doesn't intend financial lack for the church, but if you study the scriptures closely, you'll see that the Levites were to keep a tenth of the tithes personally and use the other nine-tenths for the community.

Not only are people unwilling to hear this message of giving to the church, but most churches are afraid to teach this message. Most pastors and rabbis are afraid to talk about tithing to their ministries, but if these religious leaders really believed that God pours out what I call a seed harvest on a seed offering to those who give, then of course they'd readily tell their congregations about the benefits of giving unto God! They would be teaching people to expect a harvest on the seed they give up because God is the Lord of the harvest.

When I hear people talk about financial deals and about investments that will yield a 25% or 30% return on their money, I say to myself as a financial counselor, "Who cares?" You could get 25% in an investment that entails risk, but God, in His word, has also promised 30, 60, and a hundredfold return on His tithes. As Malachi said, the blessings through heaven's windows are so great that you can't even contain them.

But we don't take God at His word. We forget to take Him at His word in regard to establishing a relationship with Him, which is simply to accept His free gift of relationship. It is much more difficult to take God at His word regarding our finances.

The best way to manage your money and not become greedy—that is, not love money so that it controls you—is to be a giver. In over three decades as a Christian and through The Safe Money System, I have never seen any givers squander the other 90% after they tithe, whether they're tithing just 10% or tithing even more.

If a guy makes a million dollars a year and he is righteous, meaning he is in right standing with God and his income was not unrighteous or earned from ill gain or illegal, oppressive activity, and if that income is the hard-earned fruits of his labor and he gives $100,000 away, then wants to buy a Ferrari, I say, let him buy it.

In a situation like that, there will always be people who judge. There will always be people who look at somebody driving a Ferrari and think that he should be driving a "lesser" car, or they'll see that person in his large house and they'll say he could be living in a smaller one. These people make judgments out of their own insecurities and their lack of understanding regarding how God's economy functions.

I have studied scriptures that have helped me and flourished me financially, but I have still yet to receive a blessing from God that is so great that I can't contain it! What is interesting, however, is that I have received from God much more than I have given. Our country has been in the midst of an economic recession for two and a half years, but I have not missed a beat financially. I've been making the same or more over the last two and a half years as I had made during the five years prior to that.

My goal isn't to tell people, "Look at me and do it my way." I aim to point people toward God. I point toward Luke 6:38, which says, "Give, and it will be given to you. A good measure, pressed down, shaken together and running over, will be poured into your bosom."

Chapter 6 of Matthew says to give to the needy without show. It says to do it without bringing attention to yourself because if you bring attention to yourself, you have your reward already. That same chapter also says to pray to God without show. It says to avoid the pomp and circumstance that will bring attention to whether or not you are a righteous person who can play the part by praying out loud. Televangelists often seem to deal with these issues. I've always had a problem with much of the praying that goes on in television. I can see how some people are genuinely trying to lead others into prayer and communication with God, but there are certain times when the spirit of God within me goes off and says, "This is nonsense. This is a show. This has nothing to do with the person's relationship with God, and has everything to do with pomposity," but I'll let them work that out with God.

In a similar vein, there's a story of a rabbi in a synagogue on Yom Kippur, the Jewish Day of Atonement. The rabbi drops to the ground, rolls on the altar and says, "God, I am nothing but dust and ashes." Then the cantor drops to the altar floor and says, "God, I am nothing but dust and ashes." Then the president of the congregation does the same thing, and the rabbi and cantor look at each other and say, "Ha! Look who thinks he's dust and ashes!"

Giving is not about the show or about who sees what. Giving is about your personal relationship with and obligation to God. You tithe to your church or synagogue to take care of your ministers and of the people who feed you spiritually.

I want to drill this in because too often, I hear people say, "I don't need to give because they don't need my money." I hear this excuse more often than anything else in the churches that I've attended. People believe this because they see that the pastor drives a nice car that he "shouldn't" be driving or has a house that's a little bit bigger than they think he should have. They size up the church building relative to its mortgage and its expenses. People are stuck on the idea that if the church is flourishing, we don't need to give to the church. On the other hand, if the pastor or rabbi were to come forth and say, "We have an extreme financial need and we need to up the ante on the offerings," people would respond

We naturally feel better when we believe we're giving towards a need, but if we wait for a need to exist before we give, then we're missing the boat completely. Psalm 112 says, "He has scattered abroad his gifts to the poor, his righteousness endures forever." This psalm also tells us that giving is not an option. It's a command. Our giving does not depend on whether we believe churches or synagogues deserve our seed.

Paul the Apostle, a former rabbi called Saul of Tarsus, was a Jew who wrote letters to the church in Corinth. In one of his letters, 2 Corinthians, chapter 9, Paul writes, "Remember this: Whoever sows sparingly will also reap sparingly, and whoever sows generously will also reap generously." Paul understood God's seed-harvest expectancy—that when we put a seed in, we get multiple seeds out. Take the watermelon, for instance. When you plant a singular watermelon seed and grow a watermelon, that fruit bears multiple seeds inside of it. You could then take all those internal seeds and have multiple plantings and a multiplied harvest from that single first seed.

This is God's economy. The God who created those fruits and those seeds is not a God who is in the one-to-one business. God is an expectant giver. He takes one seed and blesses us with multiple seeds.

The people who existed after Moses in the Jewish scriptures were people whose language was that of crops and herds. They understood that all of their possessions first belonged to God. They also understood that they needed to support the priests so that they could continue to be their representatives before God, their teachers and the people who made sacrifices on their behalf. What is interesting is that throughout the Jewish scriptures, the focus is not on the word "tithing" itself. The focus is on the attitude of giving—the attitude of expectant giving. God's people knew that giving a singular gift or a singular seed meant a multitude of harvests like in the example of the watermelon.

People oftentimes get stuck on the technicality of tithing.—on numbers. They ask, "Do we tithe on the gross or the net?" Well, Mr. Concerned or Mr. Conservative, why don't you tithe on the net? I'd rather tithe on the gross because that ensures a bigger harvest. We should be careful not to get tangled in the economics and math of giving and receiving. It's not about percentages. It's the basic understanding that the more we give, the higher the return. The numbers are details that you need to work out with God. The bottom line is that we would and could give generously to God, even out of our lack, if we truly understood God's word, truly trusted God, and truly believed the idea of expecting a harvest from a sown seed. This is the way God operates. God didn't give us Jesus Christ to get one or two guys in return. God told Abraham that through his seed, Isaac, a multitude of people as numerous as the sands and the stars would become his descendants. God doesn't say, "Give me one seed and I will produce one more seed from that seed." God says he will multiply.

If we go back to Paul's second letter to the church in Corinth, one key verse stands out. "And God is able to make all grace abound to you, so that in all things at all times, having all that you need, you will abound in every good work" (**Chapter 9**, verse 8). This passage says that God's financial blessings for you are always present. He will make sure that you have "all that you need" and that "you will abound" "in all things at all times." In verse 10, Paul goes on to say that God is the one "who supplies seed to the sower and bread for food." God is the one who gives us the little seed in the first place! Then, if we obediently offer it back to him, God multiplies that seed.

Wealth is nothing more than having what you need. What we need, God provides. What God provides, we tithe back to God, and He blesses what we have. I don't know how God can be any clearer.

This is why it is important to tithe to the people who lead us to God and feed us with the words God has for us. Sow your seed wherever you are fed. You don't go to McDonald's and order dinner for your family and then leave without paying to go across the street and give the money to Jack in the Box. If you're being fed in a certain temple or church, offer your tithe to that place. The money you give to World Vision or the Children's Fund or the Jewish Federation isn't your tithe. That money is your freewill offering above and beyond your tenth.

Your tithe, the tenth, is the "obligated" tithe that God asks you to bring into your storehouse—the place that feeds you, as Malachi said. Through that storehouse, God can take care of you in the midst of a depression, in the midst of war, or in the midst of losing a job or another financial issue you may have. He sustains you financially, emotionally, and relationally. Prosperity doesn't always mean a Bill Gates situation. It means that through God, you'll always have enough and you'll always be in balance. Your money won't run you; you'll run your money because you've managed it God's way.

When my clients approach me and ask me what I believe and what I think they should do, I never impose these thoughts on them until they tell me that they have a relationship with God. Then I ask, "Based on that relationship with God who is a giver, do you feel that you have the heart of a giver or a taker?" The answer will always be "I feel I have the heart of a giver" because that person is in relationship with a God who gives. Then I say, "Then give."

We've mentioned this verse already, but I'll mention it again. Luke 6:38 says, "Give, and it will be given unto you." If you show favor to people, God will show favor to you. He'll bring the right people across your path. He'll bring the right jobs across your path. He'll bring clients, opportunities for your kids, and open doors.

God is a Rewarder. God knows how tough this world is and He knows that the enemy roams the world with his minions to kill, steal, and destroy God's people, but God equips us with the right weapons—the foundation of the gospel and the good news that everything belongs to God and that He wishes to bless you with it—so that we can fight our spiritual battles.

Everything is God's and He's gracious enough to entrust you with 90% of it to enjoy and do what you feel you've been called to do with it. All God asks is for you to sow into the people who feed you in your community–your home church or your home temple.

As you practice this seed-harvest principle, remember that chaos will break out around you. Doubt will come in like a wave. The last thing the enemy wants is for you to understand that God desires to bless you, but don't let this deter you from doing what God says to do in His word. You've got God Almighty, the creator of the Universe, as your dad, so why do you have any reason to fear the devil?

God allows the enemy to do what the enemy is designed to do—to challenge God's word. God allows this the way a football coach does when he tells his linemen, "This is the blocking scheme. This is the blocking scheme," then goes over to the defense and says, "The blocking scheme is going to be this. Why don't you go around?"

The coach does this to teach his linemen a lesson on how to defend their quarterback. So when God allows the enemy to challenge God's word, God is building in us the strength and ability to stick to God's word no matter what crosses our path—whatever distraction or opportunity to panic. He is shaping us to become people who can say, "I'm on the verge of losing my house, I'm on the verge of losing my job, I'm on the verge of losing the last dime in my bank, but I'm going to trust you in your word, Lord, and I'm going to give out of my poverty."

God wants us to acknowledge Him for who He is—the Rewarder of our small seeds and our small faiths. God desires to prove that He is "not a man that he would lie or change his mind." When God speaks, He will accomplish it, and what God speaks is that the more you give, the more He desires to give to you.

CHAPTER 11: THERE'S
NOTHING PASSIVE ABOUT FAITH

Throughout our lives, we're confronted with a series of decisions. Decisions, in fact, are the *essence* of our lives.

Decisions come from intentions, and our intentions start during childhood. We intend to get good grades. We intend to make the Little League team or the girls' softball team. We intend to go to a specialized high school to follow specific ambitions, but our intention to do anything without making decisions along the way is useless, unproductive and devoid of results. Every intention we have, whether it is to lose weight or finish college, will be meaningless unless we decide to follow through with a decision.

This is where faith comes in. Faith has an object. That object is *hope*. I can hope—or intend—to attend a certain college, I can hope to get a certain job, I can hope to lose fifteen pounds or hope to run a marathon, but faith takes that hope and grabs onto it as if it is a completed act. Our hope, or our intention, is lifeless unless an active faith, which acts as if the thing hoped for already exists, can propel that hope to fruition.

A person of hope thinks, "I want this." A person who has faith to support that hope thinks, "I will do this." That person with faith doesn't think, "If I do this, I may lose." A person with faith always asks, "When I do this, what will I gain?" This is why there's nothing passive about faith. In order to achieve your hopes and gain the things you desire, you cannot be passive.

Most people believe that 'faith' is an inert word. They attribute 'faith' to passive statements such as "My faith is that I'm Jewish" or "My faith is that I'm a Muslim" or "My faith is that I'm an Evangelical Christian." While that vernacular may help people verbalize what they believe, the real key to that term 'faith' is what you *do* to affirm before God what you want from Him and what you'll do for Him within the boundaries of your religious belief. Every religious belief system is useless without the actions of the believer.

So we have two words that come from 'faith.' We have 'faith' itself, which describes the system, but we also have what I call 'faith-*ing*.' 'Faithing' is the action with which you obtain the things hoped for.

So how do you 'faith'? How do you obtain the things you hope for—the things God wants for you? Of course, the first step is to acknowledge that you believe in God. If you don't believe in God, then how you got this far into this book is beyond me! If you do believe in God, 'faithing' starts on day one, when you understand and accept the relationship that God has for you. I can hope and intend to have a relationship with the God-Father, but if I don't do anything to pursue and maintain that relationship, it won't happen. God offers relationship with Him as a free gift to us, but that doesn't mean that our part in the relationship is passive. Far from it. Even a free gift, whether from a friend, a parent, a loved one or God, requires the action of acceptance.

It's also possible to reject a free gift, and just as rejection is a decision or action regarding the gift, so is acceptance. The difference between the two actions is that your acceptance of the gift of relationship with God requires an action grounded on faith.

One of the largest obstacles we face in regard to accepting God's gift of relationship is the fact that the gift is *free*. We don't feel worthy of the gift. We believe God shouldn't hand out anything for free. Like everything else in life, we should have to work for it. After all, nobody likes a trust fund baby. We attach great value to achievement. We want to identify ourselves as self-achievers. We even want to say, "I achieved God's approval. I achieved my way into heaven."

If we circle back to the theme of this book, we see that every chapter has led us to this bottom line: an acceptance of a relationship with God can only come from a 'faithing' action. In order to welcome a relationship with God into our lives, we have to set aside the traditions of men, which make God's work void by putting emphasis on our work and telling us that we have to win God's approval and earn a relationship with Him. After we no longer rely on our efforts to commune with God, we then have to go on faith that God desires to have relationship with us, even when we don't have what it takes to earn it.

Once we understand and accept God's relationship with us, how do we progress toward a fruitful fellowship with Him? First, we have to find out what God says about how to have fruitful, meaningful fellowship with Him. We can't tackle fellowship with God and fellowship with each other on our own terms. We have to seek God's word.

Let's use a car as an analogy for your life. In order to figure out how a car runs, you have to consult the manufacturer of your car. If the car needs 91 octane gas in order to run, you can't throw 87 octane in there because you hope to get away with 87. The car won't run properly. If you know that the car's tires need 38 pounds, it doesn't matter whether you heard a rumor that 30 pounds is okay. You need 38 so that the tires don't wear out sooner than normal.

Unless you get direct facts from the manufacturer's owner's manual, the information you have is useless or even harmful for your car. In the same light, you could run your life based on what you've heard from other people—your family, your coworkers or even your religious institution, but if that religious institution or your parents, as earnest as they may be, give you information regarding how to run your life and how to function apart from how God intends your life to be run, then that information will be wrong and unhelpful. A fruitful, active relationship with God needs to be directed by God's word—the Bible.

Oftentimes, we proceed down a path that appears to be lined with great decisions. We make strides toward the goals we hope for, and when we don't gain those things, we become confused because we were following all the guidelines laid out by the church. That's exactly the problem. We were hoping for the things the church taught us to hope for. We were following what people have to say as opposed to what God has to say.

If you're in this place of disappointment, seek God's word for yourself. Instead of relying on others to tell you what it says, open up your Bible and read the law. Read the teachings of Jesus and the teachings of the prophets. You'll most likely be shocked as to how differently God's word suggests you pursue a proper fellowship with Him than how the traditions of men might have told you to behave.

The next step is to take what you receive from God's word and confront Him with it. Ask God, "What are you doing here?" and "What do you mean?" Then let the Holy Spirit speak to you. Open up the word and remain in a posture of listening. Then you'll hear the Holy Spirit say, "I love you. I've accepted you. I created you for one reason: to have relationship with me. And I gave you my law, gave you my psalms, and gave you my proverbs and precepts so that you could understand how to have that fruitful fellowship with me."

Accepting God's gift of relationship means you'll have heaven *after* earth, but how do you then interact with God's word in order to obtain the things He has for you *here*? How do you partake in the kingdom of heaven on earth?

I've mentioned throughout the book that it's God's intention for His kingdom to come to us as we live on earth. In the Lord's Prayer, Jesus says, "Thy kingdom come, thy will be done on earth as it is in heaven." In order to make this happen, God gave us His power through the Holy Spirit. He gave us the tools to fight spiritual battles as kingdom warriors on this side of the curtain called 'life.' We need the tools, the law, and the Holy Spirit on this side because this is where the devil is. The other side is where the devil is *not*.

We can hope all we want for God's kingdom on earth and even make all the right decisions, but we also have to be prepared to face spiritual battle as I talked about in Chapter 2, "The Devil's War." The devil's job is to steal, kill, and destroy everything in our lives to keep us from being fruitful in bringing the kingdom of heaven to earth.

In football, the linebacker's job is to size up the quarterback and decide whether to blow through the line and attack the quarterback on a pass play or go to the outside and explode on a running-back on a running play. Regardless of how he plays the game, the linebacker's job is to wreak havoc on the offense.

Similarly, the devil's job is to wreak havoc in the life of the believer—one who has established a relationship and fellowship with God. The devil wants nothing more than to sabotage that relationship, and the devil will succeed unless we not only understand what God's word says we need to do to be protected, fruitful, and victorious, but also make decisions based on that understanding. We have to seek the spiritual weapons, gifts, and precepts God gives us, and grab hold of them through a 'faithing' action by believing that these are the tools that will win the spiritual battle.

Again, in order to do this, we have to go to God's word. We have to seek out the ample scriptures that say that God sends His angels to protect us. We have to read and understand that God has equipped us with everything we need to face our spiritual battles. Most of all, God's word can tell us who God is. Focusing on the many names of God helps us contextualize our spiritual battles in a new light—the light of God's power and God's ability to win, as opposed to what our meager efforts can do for us.

The Jews possessed many names for God, such as Jehovah-Jireh, the Provider, or Jehovah-Rapha, the healer. According to God's word, God is the protector, the foundation, and the victor. God's great names and identities are gifts He gave us to claim and take hold of during our battles. When we acknowledge these identities and continue 'faithing' by actively pitting our situations against these identities, God manifests the power of these names in those situations. Instead of focusing on the difficult situation at hand, we 'faith' by focusing on God's identity. We turn to what God can speak into the situation and what God can become in order to drastically change the circumstance from what it appears to be.

As we interact with God on this level, functional, fruitful fellowship will occur and will continue to occur. Of course, there are bumps along the road. There are times we don't 'faith,' but the more we see fruit as a byproduct of 'faithing,' the more active our faith will become.

We can break this down to the ABCs of faith. Faith is based on A: our action, which is based on B: our belief, spurred on by C: our confidence that what God's word says is true—that he will manifest himself and act in our lives so that we can be victorious in warfare against the enemy. ABC: Action based on Belief supported by Confidence in God's word.

God's word has much to give us confidence. In the last chapter, I mentioned Numbers 23:19, which says, "God is not a man, that he should lie, nor a son of man, that he should change his mind. Does he speak and then not act? Does he promise and not fulfill? I have received a command to bless; he has blessed, and I cannot change it." God is the one who gives us His blessings—His victories—and also gives us the tools and weapons we need to grab them.

We also have the opportunity to pursue the world's victories as much as we want. We can spend our lives accumulating the most toys, accumulating the most women or the most men, accumulating the most companies, and follow the world's road map toward that victory, but we know how hollow and empty that finish line will be.

In autobiography, Lee Iacocca said that he's never witnessed anyone on his deathbed reminiscing about all of his financial conquests and accumulations. A dying person reminisces about whether or not he was able to have the relationships he'd always wanted. On our deathbeds, we won't say, "I wish I had spent more time in the office than I spent with my family." Choosing which battle you want to win and how you want to be victorious in this journey is a choice.

The Bible is a book of decisions. It is a book filled with stories of people choosing to go into or out of the lives God intended for them. The Bible says that it is God's intention for all men to be saved and come to the knowledge of His truth, but while we can say all day long that God's intention is this or God's intention is that, our decisions determine whether God's desires can become reality. If we don't decide to accept the good that God has for us—salvation, health and productivity, to name a few—then we won't ever see them. No matter what grand life God has prepared for us and no matter how badly we want it, our inaction can prevent us from receiving that blessing.

Does this mean that if you're sick, it's your fault? No. God is a great healer who heals even to this day, but in addition to not believing that God heals, many people also forget that God isn't in the health maintenance business. You have a responsibility to take the necessary measures to promote good health in your body. On the other hand, there are times when sickness happens despite your good diet and exercise. Genetics play a factor, the environment plays a factor, and sometimes there's nothing you can do to prevent an illness. In this case, after you first make sure that you are right with God, the next 'faithing' action is to seek what God's word might say about your health. Go through every scripture *you* can find regarding healing and health, and instead of asking people what they mean, ask the Holy Spirit to speak directly to you. The world—the traditions of men—is full of doubt and limitations and mantras about what can't be. God's word opens us up to the possibility of what can be beyond our ability to see and understand.

In times of difficulty, the one we need to interact with is God. We need to sit down with His Holy Spirit and take advantage of the relationship we have with Him. If you have a relationship with a religious institution, then you're going to get results that come from the traditions of men. If you have a relationship with God, then you're going to get results that require a God to accomplish.

We can access the power of the Holy Spirit because this is the gift Jesus imparted to us after he resurrected, as he returned to the Father. Jesus understood that the people of his time didn't want him to leave. He understood that it's hairy out there, but he also knew that if he were walking among them, his power would be limited to where he was at any given time. If Jesus returned to heaven and doled out the Holy Spirit to everybody, then the power that was in Jesus could go forth and manifest in a billion more people to fight the battle for the kingdom on earth.

By paying the price for our sins and for what happened in the Garden of Eden, Jesus helped us gain access to a relationship with the God-Father. Then he sent us his Holy Spirit to guide us into fruitful fellowship with Him.

Jesus' resurrection is also proof to the devil and to us that he has victory over the grave. Without that resurrection, Christianity is meaningless. The entire foundation of Christianity rests on what the resurrection signifies: the victory over the grave and over the devil.

The challenge, then, is to 'faith' and allow the Holy Spirit to guide you, comfort you, counsel you, provide for you, and protect you based on the truth that whatever battle you face has already been won — if that promise is in God's word. Jesus said that he Holy Spirit would lead us to God's word. Then, when we figure out and accept what God's word says regarding our lives, the Holy Spirit acts upon that word and brings God's plans to fruition. He brings God's desire to reality in the kingdom of heaven that exists on earth.

What most religious people don't understand is the connection between Jesus Christ's death and resurrection and the agricultural concepts the scriptures often use. In the last chapter, I talked about the seed-harvest principle and touched on God's economy, which doesn't operate on a one-to-one ratio. God takes our single seed and creates a multiplied, fruitful harvest from just that one seed. In the same way, we can think of Jesus' death as a planting into the ground. Jesus, like a seed, died and 'entered the ground,' so to speak. When a seed emerges from the ground, it sprouts as a plant full of new seeds. Likewise, when Jesus rose from the dead, he rose with greater power and with the intention to multiply that power through the Holy Spirit in us.

The more I've dwelled on these concepts over the years, the more I've realized why it is vital that we 'faith' in God in order to receive His blessings in our lives. As I seek God and decide that I want my finances in order or want to bless others with my finances or want certain things for my family, I see that the enemy is much more active in wanting to steal my blessing and destroy everything that I try to do in God's name. This is why I must understand

and accept the Holy Spirit in order to engage in more productive, victorious spiritual warfare.

However, because I'm human, I sometimes take my eyes off of God and begin to focus on my problems. Those are the moments that failure, as opposed to victory, takes root. When we are at war with the devil, we can't rely on our own strength and our own abilities—the traditions of men that we hear about even in church—to win these battles. Our only hope is to return to God's word, receive what God says about His character and His promises in the situation, and then act based on who God is and what God can do, and has done, to claim those victories. As Hebrews 11:1 says, "Faith is being sure of what we hope for and certain of what we do not see."

Let's say that I'm driving quickly down a steep road down the side of a mountain. I notice police lights and realize that a car accident has occurred. I'm going 70 or 80 miles per hour down this hill and I instantly think to myself, "There's a problem. I need to stop. How do I stop? I have to hit the brake, not the gas." Though I know that hitting the brake will cause the car to stop, and though I intend for the car to stop, it isn't until I actually hit that brake that the car will stop.

Actions based on faith are based on a reality that is as sure as the knowledge that hitting the brakes means that the car will stop.

Before I brake, I can envision my future reality. I know that when I brake, the car will stop. This is what motivates the 'faithing' action of hitting the brake. This kind of certainty and active decision-making is how we need to approach everything else we envision in life. Without our actions, God's intentions and desires for us will not become a reality.

God rewards those who 'faith.' Habbakuk, the Old Testament prophet, said, "The just shall live by faith." He didn't say that the just shall live by religious principles. Religious principles are part of faith, but what God responds to and what helps us function with God in spirit and truth is our faith as we actively accept God's relationship and God's realities for us.

This is fundamentally why Jesus disputed more with religious leaders than with the Romans. Jesus preached a message of faith and acceptance of what God already has for us as opposed to a message of what we can accomplish through the traditions of men to attain God's blessings. Jesus, who was a rabbi, wasn't a foreign missionary coming in to declare, "You guys are all wrong." He—like Paul, Saul of Tarsus—knew the faith of the Jews inside and out, and he saw that the extreme focus on religious traditions had begun to make void the word of God.

When Jesus healed people on the Sabbath, religious leaders berated him for breaking tradition, but Jesus was more concerned with what God wanted for his people—healing, stability, prosperity—than what people could do on their own merits. Jesus said, "The Sabbath wasn't made for you. It was made for the Lord."

Jesus gave the example of King David, who marched through a field with his men after a battle. When they were starving, they went into an area where priests kept grain for religious purposes, and partook of that grain so that they could survive to fight another day. They understood that God cared about their hunger and well-being, and knew that desire of God transcended the traditions of men.

These men acted based on faith in God's character. They didn't passively submit to the outlines religious men laid out for them. Being able to stand up to the traditions of men and face life's struggles by relying on God's word instead of our preconceived ideas of God takes courage. It isn't a sign of weakness.

People may say that having faith is a crutch, but then I would suggest that every belief system is, in some ways, a crutch. If my belief system is based on my ability to adhere to the traditions of men, then I'm using my strength as a crutch. When we take us out of the equation, our reliance on God to accomplish His word and give us everything we need to be victorious in our battles resembles a freedom more than a crutch.

When we don't trust God, it is because we are often too afraid, too stubborn, or too weak to let go of trusting ourselves. We've become dependent on ourselves and on the traditions of men, which have become our crutch.

If you're in prison, you can't let yourself out. Somebody else has to come to let you out. Somebody else has to pay bail. Acknowledging that you are in jail and accepting that you have no ability to fight your battles, as tough as you are or as bright as you are, is not a crutch. It is uncommon wisdom. To accept that wisdom and accept that we need somebody else to let us out of our prisons are acts of faith, and faith is the assurance that because of God's unchangeable character, the things that we hope for will become reality.

CHAPTER 12: THE TRUEST FORM OF FREEDOM

When I think of freedom, I recall Martin Luther King, Jr.'s "I Have a Dream" speech, in which he quotes a 'Negro spiritual,' which he says he hopes everyone will one day be able to sing: "Free at last, free at last. Thank God Almighty, we are free at last."

My main purpose throughout this book has been to shine light on the traditions of men and expose the ways those traditions void God's word. The word of God helps us establish and receive a relationship with God, and the traditions of men have warped the way we've approached this relationship. The truth is that we have been given the freedom to be autonomous moral agents who can decide on our own whether to accept God's word and accept His gift of relationship with us. Since we are free moral agents, we must first discover who God is and then figure out who we are if we want to accept God into our lives. God's word helps us understand that we are sinners in need of a savior. On Yom Kippur, the Jewish Day of Atonement, Jews receive a sacrifice for their sins and accept forgiveness. Christians believe that Christ was the fulfillment of atonement. We believe that before the messiah returns as king, he needed to come to fulfill the role of the suffering servant and be the ultimate sacrifice for our sins.

Through that sacrifice of Jesus, God gifts the possibility of a relationship with us, but in addition to that gift, God also gives us the freedom to decide whether to receive it. This has been the theme of this book.

After a relationship with God is established, the law enters to provide order and direction for us to pursue proper fellowship with God and with each other. In this chapter, I'll discuss the way that this law increases our freedom.

The quintessential scripture that speaks to freedom is in the gospel of John, chapter 8, verse 32, when Jesus says, "You will know the truth, and the truth will set you free." We often misinterpret scripture or hold on to ideas that have been passed down by religious institutions but are not rooted in God's word. For example, many religious people will say that the Bible claims that money is the root of all evil, but if you study scripture, you'll find that it doesn't say that money is evil. The Bible says that the *love of* money—greed and the idolization of money—is what harms us.

The phrase "the truth will set you free" has become somewhat of a contemporary mantra, and very few people realize that it comes from the Bible. It is important to read that verse in context to figure out what Jesus really means. Before Jesus says that you will know the truth, and that this truth will set you free, Jesus says in verse 31, "If you hold to my teaching, you are really my disciples." He says, *"Then* you will know the truth."

When we read this message of freedom in the right context, we find a huge shift in meaning. Jesus shows us the source of freedom–truth. The foundation of truth? The word of God.

The idea of freedom evolved from and is predicated upon us knowing the word of God and living our lives according to the word of God. As I've described throughout this book, the word of God teaches us how we are able to *accept* God's love rather than *earn* God's love. We can do this based on what *He* did as opposed to what *we* do. This truth has freed us from having to try to reach God on our own merits.

After we receive God, many of us begin to believe that God's laws and our obligations in our relationship with Him resemble bondage more than they resemble freedom. It seems contradictory to us that following God can be freeing. In order to address that apparent contradiction, let's address the idea of sin. Because God gave us the free will to sin, I have a right to sin. I have the ability and the liberty to sin. Sinning may not be the most conducive means to maintaining a functional relationship with God or with anyone else, but I can choose it any time.

The Bible says that the result of sin is death. Death doesn't necessarily mean "the cessation of" something. For example, your tooth or your leg can be dead, but that body part still exists. It doesn't cease to be. It just exists in a different state. Similarly, when the Bible says that you were once dead to God, but are now alive to him, it doesn't mean that you were ever non-existent to God. Just like a dead body part is useless and insensitive to the rest of the body, when you are dead because of sin, you are unable to relate to and unable to feel the power of a relationship with God.

By "sin," I don't mean saying a bad word or punching somebody who has aggravated you. I'm talking about the *attitude* of sin. The big picture is that sin is what separates us from God. The Bible uses the illustration of an archer to help us understand sin. An archer aims for the bulls-eye at the center of a target. Like that archer, we're aiming for God's perfection, but we miss. Sin is what causes us to miss the target and miss out on a perfect fellowship with God.

By our very nature, nobody is able to follow every Levitical Law or the Ten Commandments and abide by them 100%. Nobody scores a perfect 100 on this test. As Romans 3:23 says, "All have sinned and have fallen short of the glory of God." Everyone has missed the mark. Trying over and over again by our own efforts to hit that bulls-eye is a form of bondage. If this were our reality, we could never feel free to have a relationship with God. Seeking God would be a discouraging process.

Freedom comes from understanding that God offers relationship to us because He covers our sins. God restores relationship with us when we accept His act of sacrifice. God hits the bulls-eye *for* us.

In order to understand this concept, we need that active faith we talked about in the last chapter—that saving, delivering faith. With this faith, Christians believe and accept that Christ paid the price for our sins once and for all through the blood he shed on the cross. He was dead for three days when the spirit of God rose him up, took him from Satan's control, and established him at the right hand of God's throne. Christ's blood was sprinkled on the holy seat of God which, in Jewish scriptures, was in the Holy of Holies, the most inner, sacred sanctuary of the temple. Just as the Holy of Holies is where the High Priest enters to offer the annual blood of sacrifice on Yom Kippur, Christians believe that Christ's blood was the one-time blood sacrifice sprinkled on the Holy of Holies in God's temple in heaven. This one-time sacrifice means that our sins have been covered for eternity and are now gone.

The Jewish king David talks about the importance of entering into this blood covenant with God. In Psalm 103, he says, "Bless the Lord, oh my soul, and forget not his benefits." King David goes on to identify the Lord as one "who forgives all your sins, who heals all your diseases, who redeems your life from destruction."

King David understood that a covenant with God comes with benefits: sins that are forgiven, diseases that are healed. God gives us His word and His laws so that we know how to function properly with Him in fellowship. Likewise, your car's owner's manual tells you exactly how to take care of your car so that it can function at its maximum performance level. Following the guidelines to maintain your car doesn't cause you to feel *less* free. It helps you achieve the greater freedom of a functional car. The Bible, our "owner's manual" for our lives, guides us so that we can have the freedom to live more functional lives.

When I follow God's word, the Holy Spirit empowers me through his word. The Holy Spirit reminds me of scriptures to apply to every aspect of my life. Whether I have to make a business decision or a relationship decision, the Holy Spirit uses God's word to guide me in a direction that will lead to more freedom, away from the bondage of sin.

For example, the Holy Spirit can speak to you regarding whom you marry, how you function in that marriage, and whom you hang around with while you are married. You already know that the kids your children run around with affect your children's behavior. This is why, even as adults, we need to hang around with people who will exhort us to stay in fellowship with God and in fellowship with those around us.

If you are a man who wants to remain faithful to your wife, then you better discard those guys who aren't faithful to theirs and spend their time "fellowshipping" in strip clubs. It is important to find other men who love God first. Find men who identify themselves as royalty—as sons of God—and live out the reality of God's kingdom of heaven in this life. Find men who don't desire to dishonor God, their wives, their kids and themselves. Living in harmonious fellowship with God and with the people we love is where we find true freedom.

Instead of assuming how to succeed in these relationships based on the traditions of men, let the Holy Spirit lead you through God's word. If you are a businessperson, you have the liberty to cheat people financially. You could steal, manipulate, or go back on your word. You could sacrifice your integrity for a heftier paycheck. On the other extreme, you could denounce money, and like we mentioned before, simply declare all money evil.

I encourage you to dig through God's word yourself to find the proverbs and scriptures that talk about righteous wealth amassed in right standing before God. God promotes wealth. He even uses money to bless us.

True wealth from God is established by your ability to solve the problems of the people whom God brings across your path. You do this through the abilities and talents God has given you.

The exchange of wealth in this world is predicated upon a system in which a problem arises, a problem is solved, and the solver of the problem receives payment. If you chip a tooth, you have a problem, and you pay the dentist to fix it. The dentist, by using his abilities to address the problems of people who come his way, amasses wealth in a positive way. Keep in mind that wealth has nothing to do with how many zeroes are after that first number; wealth is the idea that you always have enough.

Throughout this book, I've highlighted the importance of the Golden Rule. Think about the businessman who is not concerned about others and doesn't treat his clients or his employees by the Golden Rule, spends his life confiscating and accumulating wealth for himself. He might say that the person with the most toys wins, but his life will only amount to a hearse with a bunch of U-Hauls behind it. Freedom for that businessman comes when he allows God and the Golden Rule into his business transactions and financial decisions. There is freedom in giving, and like we talked about in chapter 10, giving often leads to greater wealth! God says give, and it shall be given unto you.

Giving is a measure of wealth in the form of human capital—of love—because giving is the ultimate test of whether you have love in your life. Love was the catalyst for God to provide His son as a sacrifice for our sins. As John 3:16 says, "For God so loved the world, he gave..."

If you love your spouse, you're a giver. You're not a taker. If you love your parents or your kids, you look for opportunities to give to them and help them. You could choose a life that revolves only around you. You have the liberty to be selfish, but a life consumed by greed is a life of absolute bondage.

When we go through tests in life, whether because of our own mistakes or because of circumstances beyond our control, we have to approach God's throne and ask him where to go. When we have financial needs, cheating our way out of them will cause greater bondage. We find freedom when we proclaim, "Lord, you have already shown me where I will go, and I accept that path. I choose to do my best before you, empowered by you to do it." Then God, who is the one who has called us and reached out to have relationships with us, helps us and does it.

As we've discussed over and over again, this is where Satan and his minions will swoop in to steal your faith and joy. The Biblical story of Job begins with an interaction between Satan and God. Satan looks at Job, a faithful person, and says to God, "Why wouldn't this man worship you? He has everything made in his life."

So God allows Satan to stir up Job's financial problems, physical problems, and familial problems. He says, "You can test him—he's my faithful servant—but don't kill him."

Eventually, all of Job's possessions are stripped away, his children are killed, his crops are lost, and he suffers from boils and physical ailments. Job's first response is to praise God and then to cry out to God and ask Him what is happening. In the meantime, Job's friends assume that Job must have done something wrong for all this turmoil to have happened around him.

When God answers, He answers by affirming His own identity. He says, "I am God," and begins to explain that He does what He pleases, whether it is establishing the constellations or satisfying the hunger of lions. God says, "Stay faithful to me and I'll reward you."

After 42 chapters of chaos, questioning, whining, and arguing with God and with his friends, and after God speaks to Job, Job replies to God, "I know that you can do all things." Then Job even musters up the ability and love to pray for those same three friends who accused him of wrong. Instead of hating the three and becoming bitter toward them, Job, through God's spirit, prayed for them. At the end of that story, God increases Job's wealth and makes him more prosperous than he was before. Job could have wallowed forever and could have become enslaved in his bitterness toward God, toward his friends, and toward himself, but instead, Job found freedom by seeking God's word and obeying it.

Obedience to God's word lends results in our lives that we could never orchestrate ourselves. The truest form of freedom comes from that obedience to God's word. The truth of His word is what sets us free. Instead of living in bondage under the law, we are able to participate in the liberty of the law. What is that law? God's word—God's law—boils down to this: love God with everything you have, and love your neighbor as you want to be loved.

EPILOGUE

Although the Bible makes it clear that God is a loving and forgiving God, many of us struggle with feelings of condemnation and shame regarding past wrongdoings. I see it all the time. I deal with it personally all the time.

As Believers, we have a "glow"—an unparalleled love and zeal for God when they first accept God's free gift of Relationship through Jesus' work on the cross. However, the minute we sin, we want to give up, cave in and quit.

We often turn away from the attending church and fellowship with others because of the judgment or perceived judgment we feel from the local church.

Jesus didn't come to judge. He came to liberate. This book was written to liberate you from the shame and sin-consciousness that so inhibits us from "pressing on to the high calling in Christ Jesus". You can't press on if shame and guilt rule your heart.

In this mindset, your sins are always kept at the forefront of your mind, and you feel unworthy of God's love and forgiveness. As a result, you strive after perfection by trying to follow every commandment to the letter. You so over-whelm yourself with the "Do's and Don'ts" that you feel as if holy living is impossible. By following the letter of the law, you miss the spirit in which it was given.

God created specific guidelines for us to follow so that we could experience and enjoy abundant life with Him and others— here and now! He wants us to live free from the negative consequences of sin, sickness, poverty and bondage. He never designed His commandments for you to feel encumbered. Neither were they designed to make you feel worse than you already do when you miss the mark. You must keep in mind that the letter of the law kills, but the spirit of the law gives life (2 Corinthians 3:6).

Righteousness—right-standing with God—is a free gift. When you became born again, when you accepted the free gift, you were declared righteous or in right standing with God (2 Corinthians 5:21). At that time, you were also sanctified (set apart for use by God) and set free from Satan's dominion (1 Corinthians 1:30; Romans 8:1-2).

In light of this, how do you get rid of sin-consciousness? You do so by focusing your attention on "doing the 'do's." By concentrating on what the Bible says to do, such as praying, giving thanks and praising God daily, you'll find that you just don't have time to worry about the "don'ts."

So what are you waiting for? Take the grace of God unveiled in this book, and get busy doing the "dos" and reignite your zeal for God!

Quit INTENDING to hook up with your God-Father — just DECIDE to do it!

RANDY HAMMON

Randy Hammon, founder of My Retirement Coach, Inc., played professional baseball for 11 years, and did his undergraduate and MBA work at Loyola University of Los Angeles. He has successfully translated the disciplines and winning attitudes into his financial advisory practice for over 30 years. He is the author of *The Safe Money System*, a common sense guide to protecting your Retirement Plan money from the Wall Street Casino and growing it without risk. He is the host of the Safe Money System Radio Show in several markets throughout the West.

His greatest passion in life is helping people to discover, as he did 33 years ago after a rigid religious upbringing, that God is always ready to establish a fruitful, thriving relationship. His cost — Immeasurable. Your price of admission — the ability to accept a free gift.

Religion vs Relationship is Randy's story of his accepting an offer he couldn't refuse, and the spiritual journey of a lifetime for the reader. He resides in Laguna Niguel, California with his wife Crystal and is the father of four grown sons.

www.ingramcontent.com/pod-product-compliance
Lightning Source LLC
Chambersburg PA
CBHW022027090426
42739CB00006BA/314